OVERCOMING EXCLUSION THROUGH ADULT LEARNING

ORGANISATION FOR ECONOMIC CO-OPERATION AND DEVELOPMENT

ORGANISATION FOR ECONOMIC CO-OPERATION AND DEVELOPMENT

Pursuant to Article 1 of the Convention signed in Paris on 14th December 1960, and which came into force on 30th September 1961, the Organisation for Economic Co-operation and Development (OECD) shall promote policies designed:

- to achieve the highest sustainable economic growth and employment and a rising standard of living in Member countries, while maintaining financial stability, and thus to contribute to the development of the world economy;
- to contribute to sound economic expansion in Member as well as non-member countries in the process of economic development; and
- to contribute to the expansion of world trade on a multilateral, non-discriminatory basis in accordance with international obligations.

The original Member countries of the OECD are Austria, Belgium, Canada, Denmark, France, Germany, Greece, Iceland, Ireland, Italy, Luxembourg, the Netherlands, Norway, Portugal, Spain, Sweden, Switzerland, Turkey, the United Kingdom and the United States. The following countries became Members subsequently through accession at the dates indicated hereafter: Japan (28th April 1964), Finland (28th January 1969), Australia (7th June 1971), New Zealand (29th May 1973), Mexico (18th May 1994), the Czech Republic (21st December 1995), Hungary (7th May 1996), Poland (22nd November 1996) and Korea (12th December 1996). The Commission of the European Communities takes part in the work of the OECD (Article 13 of the OECD Convention).

The Centre for Educational Research and Innovation was created in June 1968 by the Council of the Organisation for Economic Co-operation and Development and all Member countries of the OECD are participants.

The main objectives of the Centre are as follows:

- *analyse and develop research, innovation and key indicators in current and emerging education and learning issues, and their links to other sectors of policy;*
- *explore forward-looking coherent approaches to education and learning in the context of national and international cultural, social and economic change; and*
- *facilitate practical co-operation among Member countries and, where relevant, with non-member countries, in order to seek solutions and exchange views of educational problems of common interest.*

The Centre functions within the Organisation for Economic Co-operation and Development in accordance with the decisions of the Council of the Organisation, under the authority of the Secretary-General. It is supervised by a Governing Board composed of one national expert in its field of competence from each of the countries participating in its programme of work.

Publié en français sous le titre :

SURMONTER L'EXCLUSION GRÂCE A L'APPRENTISSAGE DES ADULTES

Foreword

This "What Works" study addresses some of the most important social and economic issues of our day, and does so through a focus on initiatives that promote learning. Learning is about opening access to economic activity and resources, and for promoting many aspects of social, cultural and personal life. The renewal of knowledge and skills is increasingly a prerequisite for meeting basic needs, for participation in economic activities, and more broadly for full and active citizenship. Learning takes place through the formalised, organised activities we call "education". At the same time, especially among adults, much goes on outside through a wide range of less formal arrangements.

On approach, the "What Works in Innovation in Education" series is distinctive among OECD education activities in being conducted over a short time period (approximately one year from the beginning of the fieldwork to publication) yet with visits made to all the countries and cases included.* The focus is on specific initiatives within a set of participating countries, identified as having proved particularly effective and innovative in the areas relevant to that particular study. This focus is complemented by relevant policy and contextual information for each country.

Six countries (and parts of countries) participated in this year's "What Works": Belgium (Flemish Community), Mexico, Netherlands, Norway, Portugal, UK (England). The study is based on:

- Background reports prepared by country experts appointed by each participating country.

---

* Previous themes for "What Works" studies were; 1993: *School: A Matter of Choice* (policies to increase school choice have functioned in practice in six countries); 1994: *Schools Under Scrutiny* (school evaluation in seven countries); 1995: *Mapping the Future: Young People and Career Guidance* (educational and career guidance in seven countries); 1996: *Parents as Partners in Schooling* (relationships between families and schools in nine countries); 1997: *Staying Ahead: in-service training and teacher professional development* (eight member countries).

OECD 1999

- Visits to the six countries by the OECD Secretariat and/or consultants to the study. Nineteen initiatives within these countries were examined in detail. Their experiences and the conclusions that can be drawn about effectiveness and innovation in learning initiatives that address exclusion form the core of this study. Through interviews, learners' views and voices were gathered.

- Previous OECD reports and other research literature.

As in previous reports in the series, the country chapters that comprise Part II are introduced by a substantial synthesis in Part I, covering the main issues, trends and conclusions that emerge from the detailed national and local analyses. Particular attention has been paid in this report not only to the views of analysts, organisers and administrators but to those of the adult learners themselves.

Under the overall responsibility of the CERI Secretariat, this report was prepared by two consultants, Mr. Ian Nash of the *Times Educational Supplement* and Mr. John Walshe of the *Irish Independent*. Within the Secretariat, the responsible officials were Motoyo Kamiya and David Istance, and they also contributed to the drafting.

The report is published on the responsibility of the Secretary-General of the OECD.

Acknowledgments

We appreciate the work and support of country experts: Dr. Dirk Van Damme (Belgium), Prof. John Field (United Kingdom), Ms. Ana Ma. Méndez Puga (Mexico), Prof. Max Van der Kamp (the Netherlands), Ms. Margreth Steen Hernes (Norway) and Prof. Rojerio Roque Amaro (Portugal). We are also grateful for contributions made by consultants: Prof. Stephen McNair, Prof. John Field, Prof. Denis Kallen and Mr. Donald Hirsch.

This study has been made possible by the financial assistance, through voluntary contributions, of the Department of Education of Belgium (Flanders); the Department of Education of Mexico; the Department of Education in the Netherlands; the Department of Education, Research and Church Affairs in Norway; the Department of Education of Portugal; and the Department for Education and Employment (International Relations Division), United Kingdom.

Table of Contents

OECD 1999

Introduction

Social exclusion has become a major problem in many OECD countries on the eve of the 21st century. If general levels of material affluence have continued to rise, important sections of society have not shared in this growth. They have been bypassed, they are missing out. The problem is compounded by the fact that exclusion is about much more than income levels. Exclusion involves a lack of social belonging and the absence of a sense of community. There are grounds for concern that lives are becoming more fragmented and less inclusive. Furthermore, major structural factors are at play that threaten to worsen the situation. The development of globalising "knowledge" economies may marginalize large groups, either for geographical reasons or because of lack of access to knowledge and learning. Exclusion is a problem that must be addressed.

Issues of exclusion, education and adult learning are being looked at from a range of perspectives within the OECD.[1] The distinctive contribution of this report in the CERI "What Works in Innovation" series is two-fold in terms of subject matter and approach. On subject matter, this study is a contribution to an important but relatively neglected field. Instead of addressing issues of exclusion and issues of adult learning separately, this report examines the impact adult learning can make on overcoming exclusion. Thus far, the main focus has been on combating social and economic disadvantage through initial education and training. Less attention has been paid to addressing the problem through adult learning.[2] Yet if lifelong learning for all is to become a reality, more emphasis will need to be given to this. This report is one contribution to this approach.

In this study, we have sought to include diverse initiatives – formal, non-formal, and informal learning; public sector, community, and enterprise-based. The learners targeted by the initiatives examined are also varied, whether indigenous communities, or geographically-defined areas of social isolation, or the long-term unemployed, or workers at risk of exclusion, or others. Learning and education represent not only the means to enhance access to knowledge, skills and diplomas in order to overcome exclusion, important though this is. They are often important direct vehicles for social inclusion – individuals meet others through learning and develop confidence and new networks; communities organise themselves by and

9

through learning activities, creating their own viability. In a world of increasing frag-mentation, the significance of this direct role has yet to be fully appreciated.

Six countries (and parts of countries) participated in this year's "What Works": Belgium (Flemish Community), Mexico, Netherlands, Norway, Portugal and the United Kingdom (England).

This has produced a rich, diverse study. The diversity precludes simple sum-mary but to facilitate readership the end of each country chapter presents high-lights of innovations and issues. At the end of Part I, in addition, a set of "policy implications" is also identified, covering the following main points:

Learning works: the innovative programmes reviewed show that it is possible to make an impact in combating even severe disadvantage and exclusion through learning initiatives, given sufficient energy, innovation and support.

Value for money: these learning projects represent very sound investments, but despite this adult education is still under-developed because it is seen as marginal to compulsory schooling and tertiary education.

Funding: this is critical, but many of the most promising learning initiatives suf-fer chronically from insecure funding. Small-scale but sustained investment can be more effective than less targeted, "scatter-gun" funding of large-scale programmes.

Innovation: how to devise policies to support the evident innovative energy in the initiatives reviewed in ways that do not constrain grassroots energy and that cross conventional departmental and policy demarcations?

Relevant, demand-driven learning, no "second best": programmes should be demand-driven not supply-driven. It should be available in forms, times and locations that are genuinely accessible for all, and it is particularly important that the voices of adults themselves are heard. Informality of learning styles does *not* mean tolerating "second-best" programmes that are less than fully serious.

Leadership and empowerment: leadership is the crucial determinant of the future of a programme. It may come from outside but successful community-based pro-grammes also identify local leadership and give the participants a greater sense of empowerment.

Building individual and community strengths: "human capital investment" should reflect, in addition to vocational/occupational knowledge and skills, those that equip adults for shifting working and labour market arrangements, including con-tract and temporary employment and other forms of economic viabilities such as self-employment and community enterprise. Investment in "social capital" and in "human capital" should be complementary: policies to support networks, commu-nities and structures that positively support learning (social capital) represent very sound approaches to bolster employability, while strengthening in adults their own sense of inclusion, their identity as citizens and confidence in themselves, their communities, families and personal lives.

Notes

1. The Directorate for Education, Employment, Labour and Social Affairs (DEELSA) has published a series of analyses of the problems associated with exclusion, including the analysis prepared for the recent meeting of the OECD Social Policy Ministers held in June 1998. (see A *Caring World: The New Social Policy Agenda*, OECD, 1999.) See also, *Battle Against Exclusion*, OECD, 1998*a* and *b*, Vol. 1 and 2.

2. Adult learning was a core issue in the most recent Education Ministers' meeting held in 1996 (see Lifelong Learning for All, OECD, 1996), and more recently in an international conference "How Adults Learn", held in Washington D.C. in April 1998, jointly organised by the OECD and the US Department of Education. In terms of the relationships and policies relating education and exclusion especially as regards some specific segments of young people, CERI has built up an extensive series of analysis (including *Implementing Inclusive Education*, OECD, 1998*i*, and *Co-ordinating Services for Children and Youth at Risk – a World View*, OECD, 1998*j*).

Part I

THEMATIC REVIEW

Chapter 1

Social Exclusion and Adult Learning:
Concepts and Dimensions

Growing attention to social exclusion

Concern is growing throughout OECD countries about the phenomenon of "social exclusion" and the barriers to participation in the workplace and wider society experienced by individuals and communities. This study addresses that concern and goes on to look in particular at the important role adult learning can play in combating exclusion. Site visits to six countries involved in the study show that there is no simple answer to the key question: "What is social exclusion?". Indeed, several adult learners rejected the term, maintaining that difficult though their circumstances were, many other people were much worse or faced greater special problems.

This chapter examines what "social exclusion" means, both as a concept and as it is manifested in OECD countries today. It shows that the term is useful in helping to focus on a range of the most worrying contemporary developments. The study focuses on programmes and projects that are particularly innovative in their use of adult learning initiatives. Far more attention has been devoted to the effort to understand how social and economic disadvantage can be addressed through schooling and initial education and training rather than through adult education and other forms of learning. In consequence, there is no well developed framework with which to link learning and exclusion as they affect adults. This chapter concludes, therefore, by presenting key points for such a framework.

Different perspectives on social exclusion

The excluded do not constitute a defined group in the population: there is no single, clear-cut definition of "social exclusion". Categories such as the "unskilled", "ethnic minorities", "the unemployed" cover a range of circumstances. While the problems of long-term poverty or unemployment are major ones, society is dynamic, with movements of individuals from one situation to another. So, "exclusion" does not bring a precise target into view but a range of associated issues.

The analysis prepared for the recent meeting of OECD Social Policy Ministers in June 1998 summarised the range of concerns under the heading "policies against exclusion" as follows:

"The 'socially excluded'; 'the outsiders'; 'the underclass'; 'benefit dependency'; 'the new poor': under a variety of labels, there is concern in many OECD countries that there is a section of the community that faces extraordinary barriers to full participation in the labour market and society. The results are well known: benefit dependency leads, sooner or later, to financial deprivation. Access to public services may be denied because of lack of address or employment record. Households are no longer in control of their own destiny. Health status may be damaged by poor diet and living conditions. Upon reaching retirement, lack of contributions to employment-based public pension schemes leads to continued reliance on minimum benefits. Children grow up without examples of the normal status of work in society, increasing the risk that disadvantage is transmitted across generations. In some countries, deprived areas or even regions become detached from the modern economy, becoming unable to take advantage of any improvements in the macroeconomic environment" (see OECD, 1999, p. 100)."

This summary shows the variety of concepts in play and the range of possible causes and solutions. Some would take issue with particular formulations; for example, there is heated debate over whether "underclass" is a useful or relevant concept. Despite the lack of consensus, the importance of these issues is obvious. The passage is a helpful starting point for addressing "exclusion" in terms of "overcoming barriers to full participation in the labour market and society". It is not necessary to refer only to the most extreme cases of deprivation or isolation; equally important is how to ensure that those who are vulnerable and "at risk" do not slip into exclusion. Many of the participants in the learning programmes reviewed in this study are not such extreme cases.

Three distinct, though inter-connected, perspectives on "social exclusion" follow below: Social exclusion in recent policy debate; poverty, low incomes and disadvantage; perceptions and experience of exclusion. Each offers a significantly different focus on social exclusion.

"Social exclusion" in recent policy debate

The place of "social exclusion" in policy debate is of interest in its own right, alongside the social trends and problems to which these debates refer. Some countries and individuals are not familiar with the term, but that does not invalidate it. This uneven usage does invite the question, however, of why the term has emerged in recent years and in some OECD countries, rather than in others.

Social exclusion is only now to the fore of the political agenda in many countries, even though disadvantage has always been with us. Its recent rise as a concept can be linked to contemporary widespread changes such as the emergence of what are described today as "knowledge economies" and "learning societies". Higher skills are expected for jobs that are themselves changing rapidly. This is due in large part to the influences of the new information and communication technologies (ICTs) and to globalisation. Whole occupational and industrial sectors have been rendered obsolete with global restructuring, or transferred to other regions of the world, often with devastating impact on local economic and social infrastructures. Low-skilled and poorly educated adults are at substantial risk of long-term unemployment or of finding only jobs with low pay. The recent prominence of social exclusion on policy agendas could be due in part to an awareness among sensitive politicians and others that a large portion of the population is vulnerable, not only the most socially disadvantaged.

Despite these global factors, the notion of "social exclusion" seems more common in some countries than others – the northern countries in Europe and America, for example, compared with southern countries. This reflects social and cultural factors and, possibly, objective patterns of hardship and of family and household roles in these societies.

Part of the concern with exclusion might reflect a new public awareness: an increased sense of responsibility for society's and other people's welfare among politicians and the general public. This has as much to do with hard-nosed economic calculations as with any spontaneous rise in public altruism. The long-term structural causes and effects of exclusion are unlikely to diminish in the coming years; many governments are therefore exploring numerous ways to cut their public policy bills. There are huge financial, as well as social, costs resulting from high levels of crime and alienation, especially among the youth for whom the effects of current problems may prove very long-lasting.

It may be, too, that the willingness to use the strong terminology of "exclusion", instead of more euphemistic language, is indicative of a greater acceptance of the need for reform. The OECD Social Ministerial analysis refers to a lifting of the "policy paralysis" that characterised social policy in many countries in years gone by when the flaws of existing structures were acknowledged but fatalistically accepted. It remains to be seen how successful these reforms will be in addressing social exclusion, and how effectively they will support grass-roots innovations such as those reviewed in this study.

Poverty, low incomes, and disadvantage

The focus on "social exclusion" refers also to the realities of poverty and social disadvantage, not just policy debates. While it is not a precise technical term, the language itself is important. Some adult learners and communities visited for the study resented patronising overtones in certain terminology – for instance, "deprived" – used by others to depict their circumstances.

With this focus on poverty and disadvantage in OECD countries, the report provided for the June 1998 Social Policy Ministers' meeting addresses both the scale of the problems and those who are hit hardest. The importance of skills and education, and the pitfalls facing those who lack them, are again underlined:

"The labour market has turned against low-skilled workers, who in all countries are more likely to find themselves unemployed, non-employed or earning lower wages than their better educated colleagues. Whereas most indicators of health status show marked and continuing improvements, this is much less likely to be so for groups which are disadvantaged economically...

"Unemployment remains high – 35 million or 7 per cent of the workforce (though down from a peak of 38 million or 8 per cent in 1993) – and the risks for social cohesion have not been reduced. Unemployment remains above 10 per cent in Belgium, Finland, France, Germany, Greece, Hungary, Italy, Spain and Poland. In many of these countries, there is little hope of substantial falls in unemployment in the short term. The incidence of long-term unemployment remains disturbingly high in a number of countries. Over half of all unemployed persons had been so for more than 12 months in Belgium, Hungary, Ireland, Italy, Portugal and Spain in 1996 (OECD, 1997*b*). Less-educated workers typically experience much higher unemployment rates than more educated workers and the difference is getting larger in most countries...

"There has been a widening in the distribution of *market* (*i.e.* before taxes and transfers) income in all countries for which data are available. The *final* distribution of income (after taxes and transfers) has widened in many, but by no means all, countries. However, households where children are present are much more likely to have low incomes than they were 10 or 20 years ago. The relative position of elderly households has improved." (see A *Caring World*, OECD, 1999, p. 20.)

The evidence reveals many countries with widening income inequalities, worrying levels of unemployment and inactivity, and growing poverty, often amid a general increase in affluence. It emphasises the urgent need to tackle social exclusion. The risks of slipping into poverty and low-paid work are not exclusive to one group; far more of the population will be affected at some stage during their lives than are affected at any given point in time.

This OECD analysis confirms that certain combinations of age, gender, ethnicity and family circumstances contribute substantially to the risk of encountering serious problems. Typical high risk groups include single-parent (often mothers) families – and indeed many families headed by young adults – those with incomplete education and training; people with disabilities; older men of working age; elderly women living alone. This does not mean that all people in such "high risk" categories are living in hardship, nor that others who fall outside them have escaped poverty and isolation. Older and elderly citizens offer a good illustration – overall, their situation has markedly improved in recent times, but still very many are living in clear hardship.

The report shows too that exclusion is as much about families, households and communities as it is about individuals. For instance, across OECD countries, there has been a growth in the number of households with no wage-earner. But there has also been a rise in the number of households where at least two adults are earning. The gulf between "work-rich" and "work-poor" households is widening. There is a striking increase in the numbers of "work-poor" households – one in five households in OECD countries. Not all "work-poor" households are in hardship, but many are.

Perceptions and experiences of exclusion

A more literal focus on "inclusion" and "exclusion" concerns the experience of individuals and groups – their sense of belonging (or not) to society in general, or to their more immediate families, communities or peers. This relates closely to the growth of individualism, and fragmentation of modern life. The different senses of exclusion in this chapter are thus not identical. An individual, community or group might be highly disadvantaged but experience a greater sense of inclusion than others who are materially much better off.

Changes in society which create the conditions for social exclusion have markedly different effects on vulnerable individuals and groups, depending on the circumstances of the community or society in which they live. Where strong family structures and a sense of community and social values continue to hold sway, there is often an ability to absorb the shock of change by mutual support. This is not to romanticise or advocate a return to former times, but to note that the sense of exclusion may be sharply increased in the more individualised, isolated circumstances that are becoming the norm in many OECD countries.

Social exclusion may happen when established networks on which people have depended – extended families, the craft guild, communities with strong occupational identities, churches – break down and when nothing new emerges to take their place. Those who continue to have access to such "social capital" are often better able to withstand change. Countries where the community and family base remains relatively strong, such as those in southern Europe and Latin America have lower rates of household unemployment (OECD, 1998h), though often fewer alternatives of public social assistance as well.

The nature of communities themselves may provide the sense of cohesion. In the past, many isolated communities may not have felt excluded since everyone shared the same conditions, with little aspiration for an alternative lifestyle. They are increasingly up against powerful external forces, leading to greater fragmentation and the breakdown of traditional structures. In bolstering social cohesion, community development has an important role to play alongside other policies or programmes aimed at individuals/families, and there are examples of such approaches in this study. Yet, in our world of "virtual connection", where proximity ceases to be determinant of contact, the very question of what constitutes a "community" is an open one. The nature of learning programmes that corresponds to new forms of connectivity is equally open. The line between problem and solution can then become especially hard to draw.

As we have seen, exclusion, in the sense of measured poverty and hardship, may not be the same as the perceptions and the sense of not belonging. Families and communities may be "materially poor but socially rich". Where, however, they do coincide – hardship along with a powerful sense of isolation and loss of identity – the effects will be particularly devastating.

In recent years, social policies have been broadly aimed at providing social assistance, with additional measures to improve social circumstances and prevent a wider range of vulnerable groups emerging. Increasingly, policy makers have sought a more active approach, especially through training for employability and raising general and vocational education standards. Addressing perceptions may be just as important as more material measures. Governments will often view exclusion in a different way from the individuals, families and communities in question. The initiatives and projects discussed in this study are not always characteristic of official policy, but, in some cases, represent local innovations that have emerged perhaps to address problems ignored or inadequately addressed by national policy measures. What they share at their core is that learning, whether formal, non-formal, or informal, is a powerful weapon in the battle against exclusion.

Adult learning and social exclusion: relationships and dimensions

Learning is an integral part of wider measures to help overcome exclusion and to build the pathways to inclusion. It cannot provide all the solutions to the problems associated with exclusion but it is a very important part of the picture. In today's "knowledge economies" and "learning societies", the importance of knowledge, skills and learning for participation in all aspects of modern life becomes more and more obvious. With constant shifts in the economy, few can escape the impact of dramatic labour market changes. Learning is about opening access to economic activity and resources, and for promoting many aspects of social, cultural and personal life. Given the extent and speed of change today, learning is essential just to keep up; acute problems can arise for those who do not. Hence, the renewal of knowledge and skills is increasingly a prerequisite for meeting basic needs, for participation in economic activities, and more broadly for full and active citizenship.

But there is a major problem in ensuring such renewal, especially for those whose learning needs are greatest. Lifelong learners – whether in formal college and adult education, employment-related and work-based learning, or through their own informal learning – also tend to be those with greatest educational success in early years. The challenge in combating exclusion through learning is thus doubly daunting: those with acute learning needs are most at risk of exclusion, while being also least likely to become lifelong learners. Therefore, it is not enough to advocate lifelong learning to combat exclusion since this may exacerbate existing inequalities. Strategies and initiatives must be targeted at those most at risk.

The main links between learning and exclusion are presented below, derived from literature and analysis within the OECD (see also OECD/US Dept. of Education International Conference "How Adults Learn", Washington DC, April 1998) and outside, and from the country examples evaluated for this study.

Learning to meet basic needs

Rapid change makes it all the more important to find new ways of promoting literacy in a wider range of settings. The promotion of functional literacy is a major challenge to providers, especially as the levels of literacy required in today's world continue to rise. In some of the countries studied in this report, one in ten workers were hampered by inadequate literacy skills in their efforts to retrain. The demands created by rapidly-changing technologies mean that those adults with weakest literacy skills struggle most to keep pace.

The problems can be extreme. In very impoverished communities, many may be struggling at a subsistence level and desperate for even rudimentary information and support to improve their health, welfare and other basics. Issues of survival arise for those in desperate straits, faced by homelessness, chronic ill health and isolation in old age. Poor literacy exacerbates the problems of exclusion; it becomes a major challenge even to identify learning that is relevant to different groups. The learning needs of the community may be just as important as those of the individual. Learning can help to explore and encourage a variety of legitimate activities outside the mainstream labour market – through self-employment, co-operative endeavour, and community action – especially where employment opportunities are scarce.

Absolute gains of confidence, knowledge and skills, and relative improvement compared with those who are already advantaged, are both to be aimed for. Learning in order to improve literacy and basic skills is vital for those who need it, even if it does not promise to make significant inroads on either educational or socio-economic inequalities. High risks of social exclusion will remain, however, so long as glaring inequalities continue between those with extensive knowledge and skills and those without.

Learning for labour market participation

Those most vulnerable to exclusion from the labour market need education, training and learning to enhance employment chances. This calls for an informed understanding of their needs. It covers knowledge, skills and capacities in vocational fields where there is demand, and the ability continually to extend employment-related learning. Equally important may be participation in activities which boost confidence, broaden horizons, and promote learning skills, in arenas quite outside the workplace.

Those who have missed out need more than knowledge and skills, they need the credentials that record what has been learned. New, flexible forms of assessment and accreditation, accurately reflecting achievements and potential, hold much promise for those at risk of exclusion. Nevertheless, the educationally-experienced will often exploit these forms of assessment to even greater advantage – the learning gap will not close without the concerted effort to target learning initiatives.

Some question whether education and qualifications can help to reduce the risks of exclusion, arguing that these no longer guarantee access to good jobs and secure futures. But, it is also the case that low levels of attainment can effectively bar access to the labour market. In short, credentials are increasingly necessary and decreasingly sufficient for successful labour market participation. In the light of this, a range of approaches is needed that both enhances access to credentials and promotes the myriad forms of informal, non-certified learning.

There have been important changes to the structure and location of economic activity. Across different countries, there has been a rise in self-employment and the expansion of small enterprises. Many new jobs involve temporary, part-time or contract work, sometimes carried out in several locations or at a distance from the home by phone or computer. These call, in addition to basic work skills, for new management, self-management and administrative capacities, the ability to negotiate, as well as to engage in work-related learning in relatively unstructured settings. Learning so as to combat the risk of labour market exclusion should be informed by all these, and related, developments. As some of the case studies examined in the country chapters illustrate, this can mean supporting autonomous economic activities and self-employment outside mainstream employment.

Learning to foster social action and participation

Measures to combat exclusion should be broadened still further beyond economic activity to include a greater array of social activities related to citizenship, voluntary action and culture. This is not as an alternative to employment but because inclusion takes many forms. Successful participation in different social, community and cultural activities can also prove an effective bridge in building the skills, confidence and social capital that lead to labour market participation. Adult learning offers both preparation for such social participation and an element of it since education is a form of social inclusion itself. As the average age of activity in the labour market comes down, especially for men, and life expectancy continues to increase, these broader aims for adult learning apply forcefully for older citizens and the elderly. In fact, they are also important aims for young and middle-aged adults at risk of exclusion.

The term "use it or lose it" has been used of labour market knowledge and skills to emphasise that, without learning being put to good use, it will start to deteriorate until it is lost altogether. This applies to all learning, whether for work or for other purposes. Adult learning initiatives to combat social exclusion are valuable in themselves, but the value diminishes if learning is not applied. Realistically, not everyone will be able to enjoy "skills-rich" work environments; it is even more important, therefore, that the very wide range of community, voluntary, personal, cultural and family activities are given very high priority.

Competence and confidence in the use of information and communication technologies (ICT) represent a good example which spans the entire range of purposes: vocational, social and personal. ICT skills are increasingly central to inclusion in all aspects of contemporary life. Learning for such competence and confidence needs a prominent place in combating social exclusion.

Appropriate learning, learning environments and settings

For learning to make a significant contribution to equipping the different groups of adults at risk of exclusion, a wide range of social and economic issues must be addressed through learning that is tailored to very specific circumstances. These can relate to lone parents or women returning to work or workers at risk of redundancy or immigrants or the low-skilled. Shifting economic and social demands, changing roles and family circumstances must be addressed in different ways. People in their middle or older years may experience particular difficulties in adjusting to the "softer" skills called for today – communications, teamwork and the ability to get along with people – especially if they are mainly familiar with hierarchical structures of employment and of learning. Complex, individualised demands must be accommodated, such as for the lone parent who needs childcare support, contact with tutors outside normal working hours, and possible assistance with basic skills. Others may have a fear of learning.

There are considerable possibilities for adapting learning to this diversity of needs and circumstances. Such adaptation can be critical to the perceived relevance of the learning, which is itself critical to its success. Institutions are having to review the relationships between themselves and the learner, and as ICT systems facilitate more flexible approaches to self-study, the very definitions of teacher and learner are often blurring. Teachers in colleges and trainers in industry must review their roles and move towards becoming service and support providers for individuals and groups who take control of their own learning.

While highly individualised forms of learning and assessment promise much in terms of flexibility and "tailoring" to specific learning needs, they may perversely reinforce patterns of exclusion through neglect of social and communal involvement. Learning, through education and other purposeful engagement, is an important collective activity in its own right and is normally much more effective when engaged in collectively. A careful balance is needed, therefore, between the individualised and the collective.

It follows that the individual need not be regarded as the only "student". The case studies here show the potential for learning that is targeted at social groups, families, and communities; while recognising that these are made up of individuals. Community development schemes are reaching those who, through circumstance of history, geographical isolation or sudden changes in work patterns, have been left behind or pushed to the margins of society. Non-traditional approaches to adult learning can be explored to assist the communities realise new possibilities. The community development initiatives reviewed in this study aim to nurture mutual support, building on existing social capital within networks, families, and community interests. Adult learning can only be part of the approach in such situations, but its role may be critical. To suggest that there is a sharp contrast between individual and community approaches would be misleading. Some of the initiatives observed on the OECD visits combined both. Community development often leads to enhanced employment opportunities, while measures for employability can help foster closer community ties.

Thus, there is a major role for both the formal school, college and adult education setting and those dependent on more informal networks, community groups and electronic communication. The one should not be regarded as superior to, or in competition with, the other. The value of local innovation, and networking or project-based learning in no way diminishes the importance of formal programmes. Yet there is still a long way to go in colleges and adult education institutions making themselves more accessible to those adults most at risk of social exclusion. The next chapter describes exemplary models from both sides.

Chapter 2

Combating Exclusion through Adult Learning
in Six Countries

National policy approaches

National policy approaches towards exclusion

As governments look for ways to combat exclusion, they are reviewing both the legislative and consultative frameworks and redrawing lines of responsibility through various forms of devolution – regional and departmental. New measures are also being explored to promote closer working relationships across government departments and in association with outside agencies. The central thrust of national legislation or consultation mirrors each country's trends in policy and the extent to which different departments are expected to play a role. Belgium (Flanders) has set its sights on poverty alleviation through education and training. In Mexico, where very basic needs include clean running water, electricity and good sanitation, a National Development Plan calls for co-ordination of government and non-governmental organisations across the range of educational, health, labour, cultural and economic issues affecting whole communities. The Portuguese government is also consulting on a national plan for an integrated approach to tackling exclusion.

Measures to reduce dependency on social assistance feature prominently among countries which view "employability" as the primary goal. In the UK, welfare legislation in 1998 led to a New Deal for jobless young people and long-term unemployed adults; benefits payments were linked to offers of education, training and work. Similar measures have been introduced in Norway and the Netherlands. In the Netherlands, also, a far-reaching Adult and Vocational Education Act has defined the scope of entitlements.

Some governments perceive first and foremost the need for fundamental changes in order to tackle basic issues of "survival" which are seen as lacking often in whole communities. Others are faced primarily with what they see as a challenge to equip people with the competencies needed to meet new demands of the workplace: re-organisation and restructuring of various employment sectors and industries, globalised markets and the new information and communication technologies. All six countries in this OECD study face complex combinations of challenges at both these levels, to a greater or lesser degree, and are developing policy approaches and national strategies accordingly.

The devolution of powers to implement policy has triggered widely varying responses to problems of exclusion within countries. For example, the UK government has set up regional development agencies to take control of policy from central government. They are expected to galvanise and respond to the efforts and interests of the range of stakeholders. Portugal has five regional offices to co-ordinate education and community development.

National policy approach towards adult learning

As mentioned above, policy approaches with regard to exclusion issues are diverse and complex; many have little to do directly with learning and education. Nonetheless, in recent years, there has been an increasing recognition of the importance of education and the potential role of adult learning in combating exclusion, not as the only instrument for change but rather in combination with other policy approaches. Common policy goals include an entitlement to enable all adults to reach at least upper secondary level education or the vocational equivalent. This is regarded as the minimum access point for training and for the majority of jobs in the current labour markets. It is also seen as the level from which further exclusion can be most effectively prevented, in terms of social and democratic participation as much as employment.

In 1997, Norway published for consultation *New Competence – The basis for a total policy for continuing education and training for adults*, having identified the main factors of exclusion as "poor education, lack of skills and competencies and out-dated knowledge". The following year, the UK government published a Green Paper for future policy on lifelong learning for all. Ministers had already singled out adult learning as the means of achieving fairer and better opportunities in the job market. A similar perception of the centrality of adult learning is held in the Netherlands, which used a major piece of legislation, in the Adult and Vocational Education Act, to reassess the role of adult learning. In Mexico, adult basic education and improved literacy levels are seen as a prime nation-wide objective.

All countries have set about reassessing adult education. After an extensive review in the early 1990s, the government of Belgium (Flanders) highlighted "inadequate schooling and functional illiteracy" as the main causes of exclusion. Adult basic education was seen therefore as the most important institutional strategy. And in Portugal, a government study in 1997 concluded that a new approach was needed to increase adult access to learning and to improve the routes to qualifying in order to encourage much wider participation in education and training.

Elements of policies to tackle exclusion through learning

Education and learning

There are several widely perceived needs among those policy makers who have been charged with drafting new measures to combat exclusion. These include a new very flexible curriculum, tailored to the demands for "relevant" learning programmes in the home, workplace or community. All six countries are considering national curriculum and assessment frameworks to encompass those demands.

The roles of the "teacher" and "learner" are changing in many countries, as policies demand more flexible learning styles. In the UK, new learning materials are being produced for distance learning programmes. The role of "education provider" varies in accordance with where the classroom happens to be. Lifelong learning is becoming a necessity rather than a luxury as everyone is affected by the technological revolution and globalised markets.

Within a conventional educational institution setting, there are distinct roles for teachers and learners; teachers are often viewed as authoritative figures and the transmitters of information and knowledge while learners are passive receivers of information and knowledge. In the field of adult non-formal and informal education, the roles of the teacher and learner converge; the teacher and learner often alternate their roles.

Leadership is a key ingredient in the policy approaches of most countries since strong leaders are seen as vital in making the projects sustainable. In Mexico, leadership training is an integrated part of the projects. In Portugal and Mexico, the policy aimed at making projects self-sustaining seeks out likely community leaders. The search for good leaders is an integral part of assertiveness training for ethnic minorities on projects in the Netherlands.

A corollary of leadership is empowerment. Research from the Norwegian Institute for Adult Learning suggests that headway cannot be made in helping individuals take control of their lives until they have "unlearned" the emotional responses which are tied to failure, under-achievement and low self-esteem at school. Many projects aimed at countering the forces of exclusion focus on empowerment of groups such as ethnic minorities, women and indigenous peoples (Belgium, Netherlands and Mexico).

Service delivery

Institutions are under pressure from governments to reform their practices substantially. Traditional colleges in the UK are expected to abandon the campus and seek out learners in the community; in Norway, state schools are urged to compete commercially for industry-run courses. In Mexico, the conventional way of delivering basic education for adults is being altered. All governments in this study recognise that conventional educational institutions are in danger of not meeting new and emerging needs of learners and society. The governments expect the institutions to take on new roles such as brokers and providers in non-formal settings.

Partnership is probably the most profound area of change. As governments cut back on direct state provision, they are turning more and more to partnerships, involving a wide range of stakeholders, from employers, trade unions and non-governmental organisations (NGO), to voluntary bodies, not-for-profit organisations, community groups and education institutions. In some countries, employers and trade unions are expected to make substantial commitments to funding; for example, in Norway, the government expects a trade-off in annual pay negotiations between a salary settlement and spending on training to prevent exclusion. In the UK (England), employers provide considerable learning opportunities in the workplace, and in some countries where trade unions have a significant role to play, they have become major single providers of measures to combat exclusion. Government policies are aimed increasingly at drawing these providers into broader partnerships. In Portugal, the partnership policy is enshrined in the form of a national agency representing all interest groups.

Tools for policies and practice

Persistent long-term unemployment is one of the major issues in many OECD Member countries. Conventional policies of training people for work and then leaving them to fend for themselves are being radically reappraised. This "place and forget" approach in job placement will no longer suffice, The long-term unemployed require more than conventional service provisions even at the time of the labour market's upturn. The question of effective guidance and counselling has become more pressing.

New policies are emerging to encourage recruitment and retention of excluded and vulnerable groups on to education and training programmes and to reward both the learner and provider. Portugal operates a minimum wage guarantee for all adults without the equivalent of the secondary school diploma who sign up for approved courses. Both the UK and Netherlands operate payment-by-results schemes where different elements of government money are payable to education and training providers on recruitment, retention and successful outcomes. Cash for courses in the Netherlands is weighted in favour of recruitment from excluded groups.

As part of its national plan, Portugal is establishing new systems for advice and guidance, linked to the accreditation of prior learning, to ensure consistency between the courses that adults follow and the recognition they gain in terms of a nationally accepted qualification.

The case studies: target issues and population

Projects in this study illustrate the broad range of policy approaches by countries in their efforts to tackle exclusion. One approach is to look at a community or segment of the population with multiple needs: health, housing and sanitation. Another approach is to look more specifically at the employment needs of individuals in target groups. The two approaches are not exclusive; the 19 projects show different shades and degrees of each in complex relationships. Approximately half of these projects are targeted at whole populations, for example projects in Mexico and Portugal. Others, in Belgium, Norway and the UK, reveal a growing appreciation of the benefits of targeting a community or group in order to reach more individuals.

The complex way in which these two approaches are combined is illustrated in a project, *Misiones Culturales* in Mexico. It is a strong community-based project in combination with individually-targeted training for different trades. In Belgium (Flanders), the Integration of Senior Citizens in Society (ISIS) project aims to create jobs for individuals while seeking a community-based solution to the inadequate care services for elderly people.

Projects in this study, which start out from the viewpoint of a community or a segment of the population, tend to take a collective approach in order to address needs; examples include the work with an indigenous community in Mexico, isolated rural communities in Mexico and Portugal, and disadvantaged urban communities on a council estate in the UK and in shanty towns of Mexico and Portugal. In projects where the employment needs of individuals in target groups prevail, issues around employability are the main focus. In the latter approach, five distinctive groups have emerged. The groupings are not mutually exclusive; most share one or more of the characteristics of other groups (*e.g.* long-term unemployed women with low skills and with ethnic minority background):

- migrants and ethnic minorities, including groups suffering racial and employment discrimination in the Netherlands and Belgium (Flanders);
- low-skilled and low schooled (early school-leaver), such as in the UK examples and poverty-stricken workers outside the official labour market in Portugal;
- long-term unemployed, such as workers in the Netherlands who had been regarded as virtually unemployable;
- women, such as rural and ethnic minority women in Belgium (Flanders), single mothers in Norway, young women in the Netherlands with poor job prospects;
- workers at risk of exclusion: telecommunications and fish processing workers in Norway and factory workers in Portugal and Belgium (Flanders) whose industries are facing re-structuring and re-organisation.

Organisational features of the case studies

The way projects are organised – the locations, education and learning components and support given – also reveals a complex picture of different approaches.

Location

Around two-thirds of the projects in this study are based in urban centres some of which are highly disadvantaged. The rest of the projects are in rural areas. Like the projects in Belgium (Flanders) and Mexico, these rural communities are suffering from the outflow of the population and declining local economies. Exceptions in this category include the Mexican communal bank project which has programme in both rural and urban sites.

Some projects are wholly or substantially in the workplace, of which two in Norway and one each in Portugal and Belgium (Flanders) are pre-emptive programmes to prevent "at risk" workers slipping into exclusion. Others are in "educational" institutions such as schools and training centres. One-third of the projects mix formal institutional learning with work-based training, while a few are in local communities, not being housed in either workplace or educational institutions.

As with the targeting of populations, the location is not a simple "either/or" question but a mix of locations to suit different aspects of each project. For instance, telecommunications workers at risk of redundancy in Norway mix workplace training, distance learning and attendance at college; the balance of locations varies to suit individual needs.

Education and learning components

The adult education content of the projects studied ranges from the traditional curriculum type approach (single mothers returning to learn in Norway) to learning programmes organised on very non-formal lines, often without a fixed curriculum or time scale (indigenous enterprise and women training to run community banks in Mexico). The sheer variety reflects the extent to which project organisers have had to respond to diverse demands. Each of the 19 cases studied was highly specific, reflecting the need for every measure to combat exclusion to be viewed uniquely.

The more traditional and time-limited approaches tended to be associated with the institutional and workplace projects of the Netherlands and Belgium. But the extensive guidance, support, tailoring and follow-up provided throughout and after the study programmes meant each adult had highly personalised and individual attention.

Settings for learning activities range from the traditional classroom to informal settings such as community centres or individual houses. There was not always a clear demarcation line between formal and informal; for instance, formally designed packages, including some of those for the UK (England) University for Industry project, are used in very informal settings such as the home, public house or social club.

Subjects covered by learners on the projects varied widely from literacy, practical knowledge and skills for specific trades and occupations, to "softer" skills such as assertiveness training and awareness-raising within the ethnic minority project (the Netherlands), and team building/peer support training for women home care workers (Belgium – Flanders).

Service provider and delivery

Projects in the study showed that a wide range of people provide education and learning services to learners: certificated teachers, social workers, trade training instructors, staff in adult education centres, community workers and other staff in social service agencies, former and current learners, community leaders. On the one hand, teachers, social workers, community workers and training instructors tend to have professional qualifications of one sort or another depending on their national and local contexts. Most are paid staff of institutions or organisations. On the other hand, former and current learners and community leaders, who work mostly without remuneration, take a key role in providing learning and education services in some projects in informal settings with predominantly non-formal learning components.

The provision and delivery of adult learning in the projects range from schemes which are very much teacher driven, in formal and often institutional settings, to those which are based on mutual learning where materials and guidance are provided but where there is little distinction between the teacher and the learner. The former type of provision and delivery is associated most often with measures to promote individual employability, the latter with community and collective focus.

Again, there are few projects which approach learning exclusively one way or the other. Women on vocational schemes in the Netherlands follow a curriculum with a largely prescriptive, taught element. But, equally, they are expected to take control of their own learning in some areas, to gain self-study, independent learning and teamwork skills. Projects for excluded immigrants in the shanty towns of Portugal are strongly community-based, with group learning and where individual learners will often take control by turn, guiding programmes and discussions. There is also, however, a high level of school-based recurrent learning. Yet another balance of informal and formal learning provision is found in Mexico where women are trained to run communal banks.

Partnerships between the public and private sectors are central to helping fashion and deliver programmes in the majority of projects. The tendency within employability aspects of projects is to focus on the needs of the employer or industry, while community projects focus on the needs of the learner. The balance of the approaches varies in accordance with the level of basic needs of individuals or groups.

Tools for policies and practice

Once the adults are on courses, there is still the range of challenges to providers to retain learners' interest and commitment. There is also the question of follow-up measures to help prevent them dropping out. A variety of strategies and tools has been identified in the projects in our study: guidance and counselling, brokering, incentives, the use of new technology, funding and partnership.

Guidance, coaching, counselling

In those projects where collective needs are the main focus, coaching and counselling are integrated components to the point that they are not even named as such. Even so, support of this kind is provided continually. A self-sufficiency project for indigenous people in Mexico is a typical example of how guidance, coaching and counselling are provided by the community members themselves in a process of mutual support. In the case of the communal banks project, also in Mexico, both the agency facilitators from outside the community and the group leaders assume such functions.

In those projects where individual employability is the main focus, increasingly sophisticated guidance, coaching, and counselling techniques have been introduced. In the ISIS project in Belgium (Flanders), professional social workers provide individual coaching and counselling on an ongoing basis for women workers, during training and in the workplace. Also in the Netherlands and Belgium (Flanders), advanced guidance and counselling methods are implemented by professionals in vocational training programmes to support the learners and reduce drop-out rates.

Team building and peer support

Team building and peer support have been in existence for a long time in projects which have collective needs as their main focus. They are widely viewed as vital for the viability of this type of project. Examples include projects in Mexico and Portugal where team building and peer support are consciously undertaken in one form or another although they are not always distinguished from the rest of the activities.

An increasing emphasis on team-building and peer support was observed in those projects where individual employability is the main focus. Professional social workers (in Belgium – Flanders), or some other professionals (*e.g.* Netherlands) introduced and started to include them in the curriculum.

Incentives

Incentives for institutions and organisations: there are the incentives which governments and other funding bodies provide in order to encourage institutions to implement a specific project. In Belgium (Flanders), schools received additional government funding for the ethnic minority project and in UK the college, public sector training bodies and employers who provide training were offered incentives based on successful recruitment and retention of students.

Incentives for learners: there are those aimed at the learner such as payment of tuition fees (Norway), a guaranteed full wage for a work and study combination arrangement for ethnic minority students (Belgium – Flanders), a guaranteed minimum wage to attract poorly-educated and low-skill workers back to study (Portugal) and the linking of benefits payments to learning and training contracts. Accreditation and certification provide another incentive for learners. Examples include further and higher education credits for learners on distance learning mode in the UK and accreditation as kindergarten teachers for those who complete the work/study combination programme (Belgium – Flanders).

The use of new technology

The projects studied illustrate emerging possibilities for the use of new technology as a powerful tool to address exclusion. New technology's capability to reach out to previously excluded segments of society is demonstrated to the point that in some countries, entire policy decisions would not have been possible without it. UK plans for a University for Industry, to reach marginalised and excluded groups are almost entirely information technology (IT) based. Careers guidance systems and distance learning in countries such as Norway and the Netherlands are heavily dependent on IT. In Belgium (Flanders), new technology is opening up new employment opportunities for those long-term unemployed who used to be labelled as "less employable". _33_

Funding and partnership

Funding sources in the projects in this study are diverse. In most cases, there is more than one source of funding. They range from small-scale public and private-sector groups to large grants from governments and funding from international bodies, such as the European Union. Some projects attract considerable employer investment such as in Portugal where a multi-national firm has invested in the retraining of 700 staff as part of a community development programme.

The Mexican indigenous enterprise has accomplished an impressive level of self-sufficiency, but for all other projects in this study, the need to secure stable long-term funding is a critical issue. Not-for-profit organisations have been particularly hit hard by recent government cutbacks in many countries. Struggles to raise funds while meeting new and varied needs were often mentioned during the OECD site visits. Privatisation and the freeing-up of public-sector organisations for commercial competition are being considered in UK and Netherlands as options for the future financial viability of the projects. In some projects, insufficient level of funding is supplemented by some type of self-help activities; for instance, in Mexico, the sheer scale of the exclusion problem and the limited resources make it essential that people look to self-help by organising fund-raising activities.

Employer contributions "in-kind" other than cash support are also helping to meet the costs of some projects. In Belgium (Flanders), the time workers take for a course is partly met by the company re-arranging the staffing levels and/or hiring replacement workers. In the UK, individual learning accounts are being created in which the government, employer and individual all invest.

Local initiative and national policy

The shaping of policy and the way projects work out are not always from a top-down approach. Most of the projects in this study are locally initiated. In some projects, tensions between the national policy and the local initiatives were observed. These can be creative tensions and often result in learners themselves and the education providers persuading the authorities of the need to rethink their approach to combating exclusion and to liberalise regulations. In Norway, single mothers on a welfare-to-work scheme, who were determined to have adult learning courses designed to suit them, persuaded the authorities to rethink the education regulations. In the Netherlands, an initiative by excluded women modified employer attitudes towards recruitment, with a subsequent change in employment policy.

Where local need and national policy are complementary they also have a strong impact on the shaping of projects. Again, in the Netherlands, refugees who had given up hope of employment fitted in with national retraining policies for a new basic training programme. Increasingly, initiatives are generated locally or regionally. Self-help initiatives (Mexico and Portugal) have been shaped in line with national government approaches but have in turn led to a modification of central policy.

Chapter 3

Innovation, Effectiveness and Lessons Learned

Introduction

Traditionally, broadly defined labour policies have been targeted at those excluded groups which were considered to be "employable" in mainstream labour markets. Adults perceived as "unemployable", for a wide range of largely social reasons, such as severe or multiple handicaps, have been broadly catered for under social or welfare policies.

The projects in this study illustrate a wide variety of ways in which policy makers and providers have had to look for far more effective strategies in the battle against exclusion and for more relevant, efficient and cost-effective ways of including the marginalised, at-risk and excluded adults. The degree of prescription varies markedly from country to country, and from project to project, depending on how the problems of exclusion are perceived and defined. Solutions are not always to be found at macro or national levels of policy or its implementation. Rather, as the bulk of the projects in this study illustrate, initiatives from the field, at grass-roots level, are often most effective. When nurtured, they can have a major influence in reshaping regional and national policy.

Territorial demarcation or compartmentalised policy approaches of one kind or another were witnessed throughout this study. Examples include competition and/or tension between different government ministries and departments which are in charge of similar or different programmes. There was also often limited communication and co-ordination between ministries in charge of various aspects of exclusion issues. However, some governments are increasingly looking to move away from territorial approaches and towards more integrated strategies, providing the necessary bridges to wider social and economic inclusion.

Some of the projects in the study illustrate the effectiveness of creating new and alternative mechanisms, such as self-employment, small enterprises, family businesses and community enterprise inside or outside mainstream economies and labour markets. Almost all of these projects are local initiatives. There is a curious void of government policies and programmes in this area with regard to exclusion issues which has partially to do with territorial demarcation. Given that self-employment and family-run or small enterprises are a vital segment of the economy and that many countries have experienced growth of this sector, sustaining and supporting such innovations present major policy challenges for the future.

The evidence presented in this OECD study shows that adult learning can make a significant contribution in the fight against exclusion, not in isolation but in conjunction with other agencies, within and outside government, such as health, social welfare and employment. However, one considerable problem is the extent to which adult education has been – and in many countries remains – an under-resourced service. In many participating countries in this study, adult education has been marginal and the proportion of the education budget devoted to it is low, although the exact share of government budget allocation is hard to pin down. A significant policy challenge here is the extent to which the enormous task of addressing the learning needs of excluded can be met within this low level of public spending.

Costs, efficiency and partnerships

The problems of exclusion are unlikely to diminish in the coming years, given the speed of change in most societies from globalisation and information and communication technology developments. The role of governments is being redefined, with a shift in the balance of responsibility for funding and policy implementation from the public to private and non-government sectors. Cost is always a significant issue; but the evidence from the partnership approaches is that money and expertise, whether from government or other sources, can be used more efficiently and effectively through multi-dimensional approaches which carry economies of scale and eliminate wasteful duplication. Funding and policy in many projects go beyond national boundaries, such as those in Portugal, with substantial financial support from, for example, the European Union. The extent to which projects are sustainable in the longer term without resources such as those from the EU is a question which must be addressed in the interests of longer-term viability. As several projects show, small-scale sustained investment can be as effective, if not more so, than the one-shot, big investment initiatives. Much depends on the co-ordination of local efforts and the speed with which the marginalised and excluded feel they can take ownership of a learning and support programme that is held generally in high regard.

The evidence presented in this study strongly suggests that learning becomes effective and that learners show most motivation when they see clear links between the learning and their practical needs and when they see possibilities for transforming their lives, individually or collectively. This means that the learning offered must be more than compartmentalised sets of skills or knowledge. The challenge to the policy makers is to make sure that the "curriculum" offered is relevant to both the needs and desires of the excluded adults. As many of the projects in this study illustrate, this requires radically new roles for education and training institutions and the broad range of service providers, with different mixes of formal, non-formal and informal settings.

As efforts to tackle exclusion increase, there will inevitably be greater public concern about how efficiently the resources are deployed and about the quality of those who deliver them. The range of education/learning providers involved is diverse, from social workers and industry trainers to the learners themselves; often, the trained teacher is in the minority – the definition of role of the teacher is in any case changing. This raises questions of teacher training, of staff quality control, of the educational merits of curriculum and support materials. In the projects, there is a desire for awards, certificates, diplomas. How robust are the national frameworks within which they are accredited and what progression do they offer to help ensure that the excluded become included?

New partnerships alter possibilities to monitor and evaluate the projects and see how efficiently staff and resources are deployed. This can take the form of external evaluations or self-evaluation. But the costs and benefits to the excluded and to society as a whole need constant re-examination. Monitoring and evaluation can help ensure that policies at national and local levels develop and remain in line with requirements.

In all participating countries, overall literacy rates among women are lower than men. The challenges to women are also greater since they more often have the task of balancing work, family and learning. In order to meet the diverse needs of learners in radically different social settings, teacher and other learning providers are having to review their roles and look more towards becoming service and support providers for individuals and groups who take control of their own learning. At the same time, for individuals and groups, developing competency in self-managed learning activities will become a key for their future personal and professional survival and growth.

Innovation and effectiveness

Projects in this OECD study have broken new ground in the fight against exclusion or have identified new ways of deploying resources, materials and expertise more effectively to the benefit of the adult learner; many have succeeded on both counts. Some of the strongest influences have come from the learners themselves, as they call for adult education provision which cannot be met within traditional structures and policy frameworks.

The six country studies which follow this chapter offer a wide array of examples of innovative and effective approaches to breaking down the barriers to inclusion. The present chapter focuses on six areas of notable achievement and gives a brief overview of some of the lessons which may be learned and the implications for future research programmes. The six areas of focus are: 1) communities and groups which have created viable alternative economic and social mechanisms; 2) approaches which have helped transform the local economy and community within the dominant economic system; 3) mutual and communal learning approaches; 4) projects which tailor adult learning to the individual, the workplace or the bridge between people and jobs; 5) the changing roles of existing institutions and structures; and 6) the increasing influence of employers.

Communities and groups create their own alternative mechanisms

Prominent examples of communities creating alternative economies are found in rural and urban Mexico where women set up communal banks because there were no mainstream banks and financial institutions open to them. The alternative financial mechanisms were managed in combination with small-scale business activities, all of which benefited from tailored and informal adult basic learning programmes. Also in Mexico, an indigenous people created their own company and community service – outside the mainstream labour market – which grew to the point where they established their own economic viability. They did so because they saw bleak job opportunities in the mainstream labour market. And now, due to their success, they see no need to fit into the dominant economic structure for jobs. In Portugal too, a diverse range of initiatives for an immigrant community, outside the formal education and training system, helped create lasting jobs within micro-industries.

The effectiveness is seen in the way all three communities expressed a sense of ownership, the raised levels of motivation and the increased feelings of self-confidence and satisfaction. The evidence presented in this study suggested that the identification and encouragement of strong leadership are often the key for the viability of the projects. This was seen especially in communities where a very high proportion of adults existed outside the formal labour markets.

Transforming the local economy and the community

An equally impressive range of projects has succeeded in reviving communities within the dominant economy. New life and jobs were injected into the economy of an isolated coastal town in Norway when a telecommunications company launched a dual programme to rescue "at risk" workers from redundancy and create new jobs for the unemployed. A system for employing substitute workers to cover for staff on training helped generate skills needed to meet the rapidly changing and expanding demands in the ICT-based industry which was increasingly vulnerable to globalisation.

The dwindling local economy of an entire community in Portugal was rescued by a company initiative based on a mass adult learning programme to upgrade staff in order to meet similarly changing global demands for new skills. In Belgium, a rapidly ageing community was revitalised by an initiative to provide homecare help services for seniors and to create jobs for middle-aged women seeking work.

All the projects had a profound influence on the learners themselves, raising their levels of achievement and their expectations and, in the case of Norway, creating a "learning" community with individuals who said they had gained considerable self-motivation.

Communal and mutual learning approaches

Wherever the learners themselves have a direct influence over the shaping of adult education, mutual learning approaches, peer group support and communal programmes tend to flourish. Single parents in Norway helped create an alternative educational framework, based on mutual and communal study and support, which won national acclaim. In Mexico and Portugal, basic adult learning and essential skills were often gained though unique, mutual study groups where community members shared the roles of teacher and learner. In such projects, the mutual learning is in informal (community-based) approaches only or in combination with formal (institutional) approaches, where the starting point is a programme tailored to the most basic needs. The ideas of Paolo Freire and his focus on empowering individuals and communities have been highly influential, not only in these OECD countries but worldwide.

In the UK (England), adults who were volunteers in a primary school project, aimed at raising pupil achievement, became increasingly drawn into learning for themselves, eventually devising their own programmes. The growth in adult learning was so rapid that the primary school soon became a fully-fledged community education centre. Novel learning resources emerged as the school tapped into formal institutional structures to support the informal community programmes.

The effectiveness is shown in the way the communal programmes and mutual support lead to high levels of success and progression to higher levels of education and training. The existence of the mutual support teams is shown to have a positive impact on subsequent generations of learners.

Tailor adult learning to the individual, the workplace or the bridge between people and jobs

Up to now, in many countries, learning, work and family have been in large part segmented activities for each individual to reconcile. If an individual has difficulty in reconciling these activities, he or she will mostly likely fall between the cracks. Women often have more challenges in juggling work, study and family responsibilities than men. Disadvantaged women formed a high proportion of the case studies in this report and the results indicate that a wide range of projects has succeeded in bringing the different strands of adult learning, family life and the work place together. By doing so, they are creating essential bridges between people and jobs, and between the workplace and the home, reducing the element of luck or chance that has often dominated the job markets for the excluded. In order to achieve this, a more integrated approach has been taken towards the three strands of life; in addition, both the learning and work have been tailored to suit the individual's circumstances.

Tailoring the workplace

A single solution was found to two deep-rooted social and economic problems in Belgium (Flanders): dwindling care services for the elderly and the lack of jobs for women seeking a return to work. A multi-dimensional approach to the problem led to a reshaping of work to fit around family life. New types of ancillary posts were created within social services, helping to revitalise the community and to create new ladders to social and economic improvement for women previously excluded from the labour market.

In the Norwegian fish processing industry, long-established industrial practices are being reformed in an effort to eliminate high levels of redundancy and early retirement through industrial injuries resulting from inappropriate working practices. The nationally acclaimed scheme is being studied by other Nordic countries where similarly repetitive jobs lead to costly exclusion.

The degree to which the projects were successful is clear from the markedly improved levels of self-esteem within the communities and from the longer-term commitment to the workplace among people who were previously deeply disillusioned by their prospects and conflicts between work, family and learning.

Tailoring the learning

This form of tailoring has had one of the most profound effects on the role of adult learning in overcoming exclusion, changing where, when and how the learning takes place. In the UK (England), new styles of learning materials are being produced, in consultation with prospective learners, for a planned University for Industry. The project has been designed to reach socially excluded people with a strong cross sectoral partnership. Tailored to highly individual needs, learning packages are flexible enough to fit institutional or informal settings, big business or small enterprise work stations, and can be adapted for group or individual self-study. It is not only the learning environment but also the learning hours that have had to be considered, with tutor support to suit the groups in danger of exclusion such as many shift-workers.

An initiative to improve the lives of some of the impoverished people in rural Mexico (*Misiones Culturales*) has been long-standing but still sustains high levels of innovation. The key to success is the way the government-backed learning programmes are tailored to help each community generate income and become self-sufficient. The project also tailors trade training based on the needs and interests of learners in the community and shapes learning hours in such a way so as not to be in conflict with learners' family and other responsibilities.

Tailoring the bridge between people and jobs – guidance and brokering

New intermediaries or "brokers" between the employer and unemployed are emerging in several countries as a result of efforts to overcome exclusion. The broker takes on a number of roles, from negotiating learning and training contracts which suit both parties, to offering extensive guidance and follow-up services throughout the training period and on to the workplace.

For many excluded individuals and groups, the innovation has provided a lifeline, strengthening both their sense of ownership and control and the ability to communicate their needs to employers. The new intermediary provides a bridge, connecting learners with the workplace and strengthening existing bridges. For example, socially excluded women on a vocational training project in the Netherlands have had a remarkably high rate of success in securing work, compared with trainees in other centres and colleges. The brokering arrangements were set up by the training institution to provide the learners with an "advocate" and to ensure constant updating of intelligence for employers, students and prospective staff. It also provides a support network for new employees who had graduated from the programme. In Belgium, brokering was linked with new-style coaching to give women and ethnic minorities improved learning opportunities and job prospects. In the UK (England) too, new careers guidance services with an element of brokerage are being created by government-funded training agents.

The new guidance service has been highly effective in overcoming the multiple handicaps of women who are both constrained by family duties, often with reluctant spouses, and by discrimination in the workplace. Particularly in the Netherlands, the women themselves have testified to the powerful effect such support has had in changing attitudes of employers and in persuading them to reshape work to more closely fit their circumstances. Many elements of this service have been in place for a while but they are being more finely tuned and modified with the guidance networks reflected in national policy.

Networks

Support networks are emerging from the range of learning and guidance initiatives to create for many excluded minorities a new form of "social capital", the norms, links, networks and trust which the majority of included groups take for granted. Graduates of schemes such as the Netherlands projects for women and ethnic minorities are providing these networks. Trade unions, such as the UK public sector union UNISON, are re-establishing themselves as support networks offering new learning and social support programmes, often in enlightened partnerships with employers.

The effectiveness of these networks is demonstrated by the testaments of people in excluded and marginalised situations who say that the networks help sustain a new-found sense of purpose and self-confidence, helping them return to the ranks of the included. Moreover, learners in all six study countries spoke of wider social, cultural or economic values in the support systems.

Changing roles of existing institutions and structures

Existing adult learning support systems and structures have had to adapt to the needs of the excluded as national policies have exhorted providers to be more pro-active in their efforts to widen participation. Two significant developments here are firstly, the reform of teaching and learning institutions and secondly, the creation of new partnerships of stakeholders.

Institutions

In the UK (England), adult and higher education institutions are transforming – moving from campus to communities in order to reach new excluded learners and provide them with resources to suit their needs. Increasingly, teachers and lecturers are service and support providers who help individuals and groups manage their own learning in their own time. In Norway, the universities, colleges and upper secondary schools are changing similarly, providing more distance-learning support programmes to isolated communities. In the Netherlands, training providers in industry are forging new relationships with colleges and other centres to give industry staff and potential company recruits a more flexible education service. In all cases, the most significant shift is away from the traditional formal classroom setting to the more community-focused or work-based learning environment.

The effectiveness of such changes is clear and far-reaching: successful recruitment and retention of excluded groups is rising; the learners themselves say they are more encouraged, as the curriculum is becoming more relevant; policy makers are drawing such reforms into their strategic plans. For example, in Mexico, national policy has been changed to shift the balance from formal instruction for those with poorest literacy and basic skills levels to even greater emphasis on learning in the community.

Partnership

Pressures to respond to the particular needs of individuals, groups and communities have put the focus on local rather than national innovation. Government moves towards devolution and cuts in centralised spending programmes have also demanded more local initiative. One consequence is a rise in new styles of partnership among the various stakeholders to co-ordinate efforts. No longer tied to standardised national training programmes, employers, unions, local government, non-governmental organisations and voluntary groups are setting fresh agendas to reach the excluded. Belgium (Flanders) is forming cross-over regional partnerships. In the Netherlands too, devolution has brought new types of support to partnerships, as integration of effort across government departments at municipal and regional level have supported concerted aims to improve "work, education, safety, care and liveability". In the UK also, successful pilot programmes have led to far-reaching measures to devolve policy implementation down to regional development agencies.

Effective partnership of industry, education and government in Belgium secured funds for training which transformed the working lives of low-skilled workers. Partnerships in the Netherlands succeeded in creating lasting jobs with guaranteed training and wage levels. A social contract between unions and employers in Norway secured annual funds for training.

The influence of employers

Throughout the study, the private sector re-organisation and restructuring within the context of globalised markets were strongly felt. In this context, workplace training and development are currently in major transition. Some employers have become far more pro-active beyond a purely economic or employment involvement. In the UK (England) and in Portugal, they have taken over a wide range of responsibilities including health and welfare. In Portugal, there is a Round Table of industrialists that plays a central part in the shaping of policy. In Norway, industry, closely working with the unions, is a major provider of resources.

One very significant effect in some countries is a new enlightened relationship with the unions and a significant reduction in the old employer-union hostilities. This has opened the door to more effective partnerships and led to a greater willingness to invest in training and learning even in times of economic hardship.

45

Implications for research

The experiences and initiatives covered in this What Works study suggest a rich research agenda to be developed. Though there is now widespread attention to lifelong learning as a key policy aim for OECD countries, and the adult education research tradition notwithstanding, the research base to inform that aim remains surprisingly ill-developed. Such a base would clarify patterns, experiences, policies, and influential contextual factors regarding lifelong learning as that relates to adults. Within this, a high priority is to develop a research understanding of the relationships between learning and exclusion that is every bit as rich as that relating to pre-school and school-age young people.

The many different factors that go towards making adult learning programmes effective in meeting the needs of those at risk of exclusion, and that support and sustain innovation, deserve to be much more thoroughly analysed. The experiences outlined in this report give numerous leads on where further investigation is needed. Research on the adult education sector itself is reasonably well developed compared with other aspects of adult learning. Analysis and evaluation might most usefully concentrate therefore, on adult learners and their learning in formal school, college and tertiary education, on one side, and those in the wide variety of non-formal settings for learning, on the other. The learning that takes place as an integral part of activities that are not defined as learning *per se* – *e.g.* paid work, community and voluntary activity, family life, multi-media use – and the further impact this has for the individual also deserve particular attention. Such research will necessarily have to be inter-disciplinary and/or longitudinal.

Key policy considerations

- *Learning works*: the innovative programmes reviewed show that it is possible to make an impact in combating even severe disadvantage and exclusion through learning initiatives, given sufficient energy, innovation and support. Many policy makers and others would have been tempted to write off the situation of the excluded beforehand as either hopeless or involving enormous expense. Yet the projects show what is possible, often with modest funding.

- *Value for money*: these learning projects represent very sound investments, not only in terms of human benefit but of saving larger public expenditures later on. Despite being a sound investment, adult education is still under-developed because it is seen as marginal to compulsory schooling and tertiary education. Much adult learning is informal and is still more marginalised because it is an "invisible" part of other activities.

- *Funding*: no matter how modest, funding is critical, and many of the most promising learning initiatives on the margins of the education and employment systems suffer chronically from insecure funding. How then to fund so as to sustain innovation without spreading bureaucracy? Small-scale but sustained investment is often more effective than less targeted, "scatter-gun" funding of large-scale programmes. Evaluation – that is rigorous, imaginative and matched to the true nature of the different initiatives – can offer the informed basis to judge which initiatives are working and deserve more secure funding.

- *Innovation*: there is enormous innovative energy evident in the initiatives reviewed. The challenge is now to devise policies to support this type of innovation, in ways that do not constrain grassroots energy and that cross conventional departmental and policy demarcations. Partnerships and horizontal approaches, crossing education, training, labour market, social policy and community development, are essential.

- No *"second best"*: there is clear need to address and improve teacher/trainer training, curriculum development, quality control, and inappropriate or inaccessible learning materials in many adult learning programmes. Informality *does not* mean tolerating "second-best" programmes that are less than fully serious. Enormous efforts have gone into the programmes/initiatives reviewed in this study to ensure that they really do meet learners needs, often with the intense involvement of the learners themselves.

- *Relevant, demand-driven learning*: for learning programmes to be effective they must be relevant to the wide needs and interests of the different groups at risk of exclusion, and *must be seen to be relevant to learners*. This is a considerable challenge for programme design and delivery, for it is far more demanding than putting together courses of compartmentalised, subject-dominated knowledge. Programmes should be demand-driven, not supply-driven. Guidance services have a key role in assisting the individual make appropriate choices. For learning to be demand-driven and geared to the needs of adults, it is particularly important that adults themselves are heard – especially those at risk of exclusion.

- *Tailoring to individual needs*: "tailoring" is vital too in ensuring that learning is available in forms, times and locations that are genuinely accessible for all these different individuals and groups. Child-care facilities are often a crucial consideration for mothers wishing to participate in programmes.

- *Leadership and empowerment*: leadership is the crucial determinant of the future of a programme, especially in the initial stages. In some, this leadership may come from outside with ideas that work but successful community-based programmes also identify local leadership and allow it to grow

47

and develop. Many of the more successful projects in this study also gave the participants a greater sense of control over their lives and this empowerment, in turn, benefited their families and communities. They participated actively, not passively, in the programmes which adapted to their needs and suggestions.

– *Building individual and community strengths*: it is important to invest in "human capital" – employment-enhancing knowledge, skills and competence – which is so important for those at greatest risks of exclusion. But, "social capital" – participation in networks, contact chains, and community structures – is equally important. The initiatives reviewed in this study demonstrate how both elements are needed, both in drafting overall policies and in devising initiatives to tackle exclusion.

– *New work-related learning* as part of "human capital investment" should reflect, in addition to vocational/occupational knowledge and skills, those that equip adults for shifting working and labour market arrangements: self-employment, community enterprise, contract and temporary employment. A major competence for adults to develop is knowing how to invest in one's own human resources in such less structured settings.

– *The importance of social capital*: adult learning both fosters "social capital" and depends upon it. When learning initiatives build on established networks and communities, it is embedded much more firmly in people's lives and communities. This is crucial for those at risk of exclusion. Investment in "social capital" and in "human capital" are not mutually exclusive but complementary. Policies to support networks, communities and structures that positively support learning represent very sound approaches to bolster employability. Moreover, they strengthen in adults their own sense of inclusion, their identity as citizens and confidence in themselves, their communities, families and personal lives.

Part II
COUNTRY CHAPTERS

BELGIUM

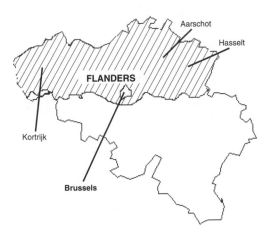

Total population (1996): 10 157 000
– age structure of population 15-64
(1995): 66.0%;
– age structure of population 65 and over
(1995): 16.1%.

Land size area: 31 000 sq km.

Per capita GDP (1996 prices): US$26 409.

Annual percentage growth rate (1997): 2.7%.

1997 unemployment rate: 9.2%
– proportion unemployed for 12 months or
more: 60.5%.

**Expenditure on education per student
(1995):** US$4 694.

**Percentage of population aged 25-64 with
at least upper secondary education:** 53%.

Sources: OECD (1998*h*), *Employment Outlook*;
"OECD in Figures – 1998"; OECD (1998*g*),
Education at a Glance.

"I'm 32 years old and a mother of two children, my husband is self-employed. Since my second child was born five years ago, I wanted to start a new career. One day, I read in the newspaper that ISIS (Integration of Senior Citizens in Society) was recruiting for part-time volunteers. It is possible to combine this job with my family life. With the support of my personal ISIS coach, I readjusted my hours to fit my family situation. The work gives me satisfaction; ISIS is a fine organisation for seniors and the community."

A mother commenting on how a community development project to help senior citizens generated paid employment for otherwise socially excluded adults.

Note: While the data above are for Belgium as a whole, the following study is limited to Flanders (the area shaded in the map).

Belgium (Flanders)

Context

Belgium is a small country and one of the most densely populated in Europe. Ten million people are crowded into 30 000 sq. kilometres of land. The geography reflects this; cities, towns and suburbs make up the vast majority of the landmass with no remote rural areas except in the Walloon provinces. The country is divided into three regions ("gewesten"): Flanders has 58 per cent of the population, the Walloon region has 32 per cent and the capital region of Brussels has 10 per cent. There are three distinctive Communities ("gemeenschappen"): Flanders (Dutch speaking people in the Flemish part and in Brussels), the French community (French-speaking people in the Walloon region and in Brussels) and a small German speaking community. Dutch is slightly more widely spoken than French; and German is spoken by fewer than 1 per cent of the population.

There are 1 million immigrants, substantially Turkish and Moroccan communities which came across in the economic boom of the 1960s and 1970s.

Despite a dramatic decline in manufacturing throughout the 1980s, Belgium is a wealthy nation with a net national income per capita in 1997 of US$26 541. The decline was matched by a rise in service industries, which account for 71 per cent of employment in all three regions. Small and medium-sized enterprises are also important to the Belgian economy.

Unemployment rates in Belgium are nonetheless among the highest in OECD countries. The 1997 OECD *Economic Surveys of Belgium and Luxembourg* shows a rate of around 9.5 per cent in Belgium for 1996. The same report argues, however, that using national definitions the figure is closer to 13 per cent and that special measures to remove the very old and the young from the registered labour force have deflated the true figures. (Statistics for this chapter are drawn from national data, while the CERI study was conducted solely on Flanders.)

Problems of exclusion in Belgium (Flanders)

Poverty is the first measure of exclusion in a country as well-off as Belgium, partly because the very deprived are in such a small minority and are acutely aware of their position. Approximately 6 per cent of the population is considered to be living in poverty. But there is a well-developed social security system which assures a minimum income. In addition to national social security, there is a social welfare system, at municipal level, for a range of needs including additional support for the unemployed. The number of people receiving social welfare is steadily growing. The causes of the increase have yet to be clearly pinpointed.

Approximately 1 million adults – 60 per cent of them women – are out of work. Belgium has the second highest rate of long-term unemployment of OECD countries, and six out of ten jobless people can expect to be out of work for at least 12 months. There are strong regional differences which leave many minorities – ethnic groups, the disabled and low schooled – in the most economically depressed areas almost permanently excluded. (In Belgium, the term "low schooled" is used for those who finished initial education with, at best, the lower secondary school diploma.)

Poor levels of literacy, particularly among the long-term unemployed, are a major problem. The *International Adult Literacy Survey* (OECD and Statistics Canada, 1997) revealed that 42 per cent of the unemployed in the Flemish Community performed at the lowest literacy skill level. However, educational standards among the unemployed are improving. In the 1970s, the bulk of people out of work had only primary education. Now at least half have a secondary school certificate. These facts reflect the very rapid growth in take-up of education. The majority of older Belgians, at school before the Second World War, had left school by the age of 14.

Age is, therefore, another significant factor affecting exclusion. Not only is low educational attainment disproportionately high among the elderly, this group also makes low demands for adult and continuing education. Belgium has a rapidly ageing population profile. Disappearance of the extended family and vanishing traditional support systems are pushing the elderly to the margins of society. New systems of care for the elderly and self-help programmes are being looked at to replace the old structures (case study No. 1).

Groups such as the physically and mentally disabled, women, low-schooled, the low-skilled, and the elderly feature disproportionately, not only among the unemployed but also the under-employed. They are the most likely to be in low-pay, low-skill, part-time jobs at the margins of the labour market. Many of the

unemployed see themselves as "vulnerable" or "marginalised" relative to the labour market rather than "excluded."

About 10 per cent of the Belgian population is ethnic minority, mainly the families and descendents of migrant workers from the Mediterranean, particularly Turkey and Morocco, who came to Belgium for manual and semi-skilled jobs in the 1950s and 1960s. The second wave of immigration in the early 1970s ended when immigration controls were imposed in 1974, reducing the inward flow to a trickle of relatives, political refugees and seasonal workers.

Closure of the coal mines caused terrible social and economic deprivation, particularly among the Turkish immigrants. The result is high and long-term unemployment among ethnic minorities much more than for the population as a whole. The search for solutions continues today (case study No. 2). Educational attainment among ethnic minorities is lower than the national average. Given its concentration, limited interaction with other sections of society and different culture and language, this section of population seems to possess the strongest sense of exclusion of all groups within the Belgian society. There is also considerable social and economic discrimination by the mainstream population.

Adult education and social exclusion

The history of adult education in Belgium is one of individual advancement as well as social and cultural emancipation. There is a long tradition of personal improvement. This type of learning has its origins in the adult evening classes and Sunday schools of the mid-nineteenth century. These schools provided elementary training in reading and writing and some vocational training for young adults who had not finished elementary school. When compulsory education was introduced in 1914 there was already a high level of attendance at elementary school. The emergence of technical schools and vocational education in the twentieth century continued the system of adult evening classes, which remain popular venues for further vocational training and professional reskilling. University extension classes were established at the end of the nineteenth century, but failed to survive the first World War, so that in Belgium there are no specific opportunities for adults in universities and institutes for higher education. Outside the formal education system, folk high schools provided opportunities for self-improvement in the post-war period. And building upon older experiences a correspondence course system was established in 1959, offering courses to prepare adults for secondary school diplomas and examinations to enter the civil service. These courses proved to be extremely popular, attracting 50 000 people a year in Belgium, but the drop-out rate was high.

Social emancipation and cultural enlightenment were powerful motives in the history of adult education in Belgium and emerging social movements had a strong interest in popular education. The Flemish Movement, for example, striving since the mid-nineteenth century for the nationalistic emancipation of the Flemish people, language and culture, gave birth to a number of very important and still functioning educational organisations. Influential educational associations grew out of the labour movements of the late nineteenth century, both social-democratic and Christian-democratic. The associative model was and still is dominant: networks of local clubs with various functions within the local community but with education as one of its central activities. These decentralised associations, however, were linked to political structures, unions and the Catholic Church in a typical manner which is labelled in Flanders as *"verzuiling"* ("pillarization") and which is responsible for a kind of socio-cultural separation in local communities. The *Socialistische Vooruitziende Vrouwen* (Provident Socialist Women) for example, founded in 1911, stated as its goal "to educate women and defend the moral and material interests of the family and to endeavour to win women to the socialist way of thinking".

Organisations active in the field of adult education also had a strong interest in cultural enlightenment of the masses. Popular libraries, theatre, music, and the spread of literature were among the activities of many associations. Making culture widely accessible and available remains a goal.

The federalisation of the Belgian state in 1970, 1980 and 1988 had a strong impact on adult education. Responsibility for large sections of the adult education landscape was transferred to regional governments at a early stage, so that the French and Flemish communities took very different paths. In the French community, the dominant socialists wanted "cultural democracy" with active intervention by the public authorities. The Catholic movements (dominant in Flanders) introduced the concept of "subsidiarity", whereby private initiative had priority of public intervention in areas of spiritual interest such as education and culture. In Flanders, this attitude is reflected in the importance of private initiatives and associations, which nevertheless are subsidised by the local and regional governments. The high level of involvement of industry and social partners in vocational education and training today reflects this.

Despite the wealth of organisations and courses available and a strong push from both the private and public side, the majority of people participating in adult education were middle class and rather well educated. Although it was functional in fostering social integration and social cohesion at the local level, adult education therefore had no real relevance to the struggle against social exclusion until the late 1970s. In the 1980s, in the context of economic decline and rising unemployment, there grew an increasing interest in the education and training of

the jobless, under-employed and the low schooled. Inspired by British and Dutch precursors a literacy movement developed in Flanders, which established literacy classes for functionally illiterate people. In 1991, the Flemish government took an important step by giving adult basic education centres a legal framework and subsidies. Also in the 1980s interest grew in vocational education for the unemployed and low schooled. A number of projects by private initiatives, company training departments, unions and the public employment and training service were established which aimed at the vocational retraining of low-skilled unemployed.

Main policy approaches

Belgium's government structure is complex; there are intricate jurisdictional divisions of responsibilities at different levels of governments. A decentralised federal system gives each of the three communities autonomy over education, employment policy and other aspects of social policies, while the federal level of government has control over social security and the welfare system. Policy approaches to the problems faced by excluded groups fall within three areas: poverty alleviation, employment initiatives and education and training measures.

Three authorities in the Flemish Community are broadly responsible for the funding and provision of adult education: the Department of Education, the Flemish Service for Employment and Vocational Training (under the Department of Employment) and the Department of Culture. One vital segment of the Belgian labour market – the self-employed – comes under a separate jurisdiction, the Department of Economic Affairs.

The Flemish government is in charge of legislation and funding, while service providers are in charge of curriculum and standard setting for teacher qualifications. There is no centralised system of examinations – the schools themselves are responsible for examinations and the awarding of diplomas. The most recent figures show that out of the total Department of Education budget of BF 245 billion, only BF 4 billion are spent on adult education, although pressure is on the government to increase the amount. However, additional indirect funding comes from the employment services and vocational education agencies. The government in Flanders took the view that inadequate schooling and functional illiteracy were the prime causes of deprivation and social exclusion; therefore, adult basic education was seen as the most important institutional weapon in the struggle against exclusion. But concerns overall remain that adult education in Flanders is too scarce, the exam and certification system too inflexible and the curriculum inadequate to meet new and growing needs in society.

_57_

Policy approaches in the 1990s were to be a continuation of the historical patterns of provision. The advantage now was that after a period of stagnation in the 1970s and 1980s, vocational training for young adults had undergone renewed expansion, giving the authorities greater scope to attend to the needs of minorities. Also, essential general education provision for adults was improved in 1990, when a decree gave official status to the adult basic education centres which had grown out of the literacy movement of the 1970s. The decree guaranteed that people with low skills or inadequate education would have open access to 29 centres which were under the authority of the Department of Education in Flanders. Foreign nationals such as immigrants and their families were offered Dutch as a second language as part of a range of new courses for vulnerable and marginal groups. The open-door policy attracts 13 000 people a year with low educational attainment.

The Department is also responsible for Education for Social Promotion or *onderwijs voor sociale promotie* (OSP) which attracts 150 000 people a year for technical and vocational education. The OSP institutions are extensions of the secondary technical schools and offer evening classes to upgrade a range of technical and language qualifications. Within OSP, there are also some schools which provide second-chance education, offering courses leading to full secondary education diplomas. These schools originated in the women's movement which lobbied for a fairer deal on education in the 1970s and 1980s.

The second area of responsibility is with the Department of Labour which has concentrated its efforts on the long-term unemployed and low-skilled. Approximately 30 000 unemployed people are on training schemes, of whom 70 per cent are long-term unemployed. Additional work experience has been added to programmes which have been expanded into the private sector (case study No. 4). The Flemish Service for Employment and Vocational Training or the *Vlaamse Dienst voor Arbeidsbemiddeling en Beroespopleiding* (VDAB), is an autonomous specialist agency in the public sector. It is responsible for ensuring that functional training is provided for both the unemployed and employed people in groups considered to be at risk of exclusion. There are 12 regional committees, representing the employers and employees, whose main function is to determine service and training allocation based on local labour market indicators. VDAB programmes are designed to meet the needs; typical programmes are those specifically for migrants such as language and job search skills training. The Department of Labour funds workplaces for those who require sheltered employment.

The third strand in the recent policy development has been an expansion of social and cultural education in associations and folk high schools. This covers non-formal learning, recreation, social networking, cultural studies and popular education. Some of these courses have been targeted at deprived areas but they remain largely middle and upper-class activities.

Policy makers have taken considerable strides towards ensuring a broad partnership approach in their efforts to combat exclusion. The government in the late 1980s encouraged employers to view themselves as substantial stakeholders. This was consolidated in the 1990s without marginalising the trade unions, which have 90 per cent of the workforce in membership, and are viewed as social partners. Like the church groups and associations, unions have played a formative role lobbying for and shaping adult learning as well as promoting wider social and community projects.

Case studies

Case study 1

Project: flexible work opportunities (home care for the elderly) for unemployed mid-life women.

Starting date: 1997.

Organisation in charge (service provider): integration of Senior Citizens in Society (ISIS) – not-for-profit organisation.

Location: Southern Limburg.

A unique project to provide the elderly with homecare involved shaping the training and work around the needs of women seeking employment. The result was the creation of a community development programme with new-style paid employment in social work.

Overview

Limburg is a suburban community in the eastern-most part of Belgium (Flanders), bordering the Netherlands. The local economy is depressed, resulting in high levels of unemployment – much of it long-term – and an exodus of young people to the cities. Women, especially those with low educational attainment, comprise one of the major groups of the long-term unemployed.

The region has an ageing population profile which leads to increasing demands being made on limited welfare services. Places in residential homes for elderly people are in short supply and there is a waiting list for home-care help.

As in many parts of Europe, Belgium has seen a disintegration of traditional family structures which used to involve the younger generation in looking after the elderly. Isolation, loneliness and dependency have become major problems for the elderly as informal care in the community has also declined.

Projects

Integration of Senior Citizens in Society (ISIS) took up the challenge of increasing the skills of people who were not already in paid employment and encourage them to take on the role of caring for the elderly, wherever the established professional services could not provide a fully flexible service, particularly at night and during holidays. Professional providers were also unable to respond fast enough to local demand for chores to be done.

One answer was to use the professional social workers to help train and provide support for local unemployed adults who would take on new jobs as ancillary staff. Such staff, it was believed, would be better placed to respond to local need more cost-effectively.

Originally started as a Christian Labour Union initiative, ISIS soon became a not-for-profit organisation, though ties are maintained and the union is involved on the board. The integration programme is a pilot project and was eight months old at the time of the OECD visit. ISIS runs two main programmes, the best-developed being the home-care service programme which now complements established social and community agencies in the area. Women participating in the first wave of recruitment were aged between 30 and 50 years.

Job opportunities as home-care workers were offered to unemployed women who had no specific medical or nursing background. The jobs were open to anyone, regardless of age or educational attainment. Many women were seeking a route back to work, having found themselves marginalised from the labour market for various reasons: a depressed local economy, long-term absence from work due to family commitments, and low educational attainment.

For these women workers, considerable stress was put on teamwork. As an aid to team building and peer support, women workers held small group meetings twice a month. A staff meeting was held once a month in order jointly to discuss their work schedules and any other issues. Each worker had a social worker as supervisor who gave individual coaching twice a month.

The other main ISIS initiative is the programme for younger seniors (age 50 and over). The emphasis is on preventive care through social integration. The programme aims to help women develop the independence and self-help skills, to cope at home. The programme was still in a formative stage at the time of the OECD visit, though it was seen as an initiative with great promise.

Social workers provide services for the seniors and for home-care ancillary workers. They ensure not only that the standards of services are maintained but also provide professional skills and knowledge in counselling and group work, including guidance, coaching, supervision, help with team building and peer support.

Half the project's funds come from the Flemish government which pays for those low-schooled, long-term unemployed. The rest is financed by charges to the seniors, who pay according to their level of income. At the time of our visit, ISIS had applied for support from the European Union's project funding.

Outcomes

The training and employment of women as ancillary home-care staff alongside the social workers proved to be an effective low-cost alternative to professional services. It is a job the women have welcomed: nine out of ten recruited in the first wave have remained in their posts. Those who made the decision not to continue often did so because of resistance at home, such as husbands objecting to their doing the work, rather than because of the work itself.

The central philosophy of the ISIS programme is that it is as important to adapt jobs to the people as it is to adapt people to the work, the latter being the more conventional approach to training for jobs. From the employee point of view, this was an important reason why the programme was a success. Flexible arrangements at ISIS for women make it easier than is usually the case at work for them to balance both job and family responsibilities.

From the viewpoint of the client (the elderly), the ISIS approach is a holistic one, treating the needs of the person in their entirety, rather than taking a fragmented approach to the services provided.

Another ISIS innovation is on-going coaching and team building. The women themselves regard the continuous support from the supervisors and peers as key to their success at work.

The women working and learning on the project gained valuable work opportunities which helped them develop work-related skills through guidance and the team approach. They saw working directly with seniors as rewarding and they liked the flexibility to fit work schedules around family responsibilities. The programme has created possibilities for women with families to gain long-lasting employment with education, training and opportunities for improvement.

Case study 2

Project: Kindergarten teacher training (work and study combination) for an ethnic minority group.

Starting date: 1993, scheduled to be folded in June 1998.

Organisation in charge: Hogeschool (publicly funded tertiary college).

Location: Hasselt, Limburg.

A migrant community in an economically-depressed former mining region achieved a breakthrough in improved race relations in a project where teachers were given special support and training to bridge the cultural divide.

Overview

Closure of the coal mines in the Hasselt district of Limburg led to an employment crisis among ethnic minority workers. Migrants, largely from Turkey and Morocco, were recruited to work the mines in the prosperous 1960s. By the 1980s, the whole industry was in rapid decline. The workers' families and descendants now account for about 60 000 people (8 per cent of the local population). Most of them are concentrated in a certain section of the city and interaction with the wider community is limited. The local economy is depressed and many of the first generation migrants are out of work. Overall, job opportunities for ethnic minorities in the region are grim: domestic work, menial tasks or low-skilled jobs such as hairdressing (for women) or employment as mechanics (for men). Children under-achieve in schools where they tend to be in the vocational diploma stream, leaving them fewer chances to pursue higher education.

Initiatives taken in order to meet minority needs in the health and education sector included employing "intercultural workers". These workers were introduced in the early 1980s to bridge the cultural differences and serve the needs of ethnic minorities in schools (nurseries and kindergartens), guidance centres, hospitals and other health service agencies. Their work was rather loosely-defined; each agency used them the way it saw fit, usually with some on-the-job training. Recruits needed no specific qualifications and were paid a minimal wage.

The project is a redesigned teacher training programme to meet the needs of the minority communities and then use the courses to upgrade the jobs of people already working with minorities as intercultural workers. Training to teach in kindergarten or any other age up to lower secondary level is a three-year programme after completion of the higher secondary school certificate. There were three teacher training schools in this region and two of them agreed to mount five-year programme of part-time courses combining the teacher training studies with intercultural work experience.

Projects

The project for ethnic minorities in Hasselt focused on training of kindergarten teachers. Regular diploma courses were modified to include a curriculum tailored to the needs of the trainees. All the recruits were those who had already worked as inter-cultural workers. In this project, they spend half the week in college and half as inter-cultural workers in the kindergarten. Continuous coaching was given in a range of support programmes, from the development of study skills and use of time manage-ment to Dutch as a second language. The idea was that the new-style kindergarten teachers, with an ethnic minority background and work experience as intercultural workers, could assume an important role to prevent the early process of exclusion and marginalisation in schools, gradually bringing about a multi-cultural mix.

Eighteen second-generation migrant women in their early to mid-20s joined the Hasselt programme in 1993 and 13 remained to the end (11 Turkish, one Moroccan and one Italian). They earned full pay while working part-time, and were promised two years seniority on taking a full teaching job after the programme. The school pro-vided accommodation and teaching staff, while support from the Department of Edu-cation included funds for a co-ordinator to provide special coaching for trainees.

Outcomes

This project was said to be a one-shot attempt: the recruits of 1993 were the only intake, there were no subsequent intakes to the programme during the past five years. The project was concluded in June 1998 as the class of 1993 graduated. During the OECD visit, reasons given for discontinuing the programme were that an increasing number of ethnic minority students were entering into mainstream post-secondary education, and similar programmes had been developed for some other occupations (such as marketing) in other schools, though the intercultural component does not seem to be included in these programmes. Lack of interest among participating schools was also cited as a reason.

The termination of this project is worth a close appraisal. Given the increasing demands from the minority communities and initial positive outcomes of the project, the termination appears to be a reflection of rather weak interest in minority policies in Belgium (Flanders). It also has to do with lack of political commitment on the part of policy makers and service providers, which could leave the minority community without the support that is crucial for continued multi-cultural development.

The ethnic minority community in Belgium is in transition. On the one hand, there is still a strong tradition of cultural norms, including very specific views on the place of women in society. Some students felt that the limited support from their spouses and family members had to be overcome in order to continue their work and study. On the other hand, the teacher training students were seen as their community's new hope and role model: women pursuing higher education for a secure, mainstream job. This has to be viewed within the context of minority communities where many first generation (predominantly male) workers are long-term unemployed and face poor prospects for the future. There have been increasing demands in the community for this type of programme.

Overall, the important bridging functions of intercultural workers for schools and for the minority communities are well recognised and their role is gaining an increasing understanding in the community at large.

Relations between the schools and migrant communities improved and there were the first signs of moves towards the sought after improved multi-cultural approach in schools. Of those who dropped out, five did so because of family or professional reasons, rather than an inability to follow the material. Occasionally the problem was the lack of adequate support from the spouse.

Nevertheless, the students were very proud of their own accomplishment and with their ability to balance work, study and responsibilities at home with limited support from their spouses and family members.

The teachers who were training the kindergarten teachers/intercultural workers were very positive about how enriching it had been teaching this group, in part because the students provided feedback. The students said the work/study combination was an effective and enriching experience and that intensive coaching and peer support were the key to their continued efforts over the five years.

Some students expressed concern and frustration, given the overall depressed state of the local economy, that kindergarten jobs would be scarce and that few posts would be available for new teachers. They believed they would be discriminated against. To this end, the real outcome of the project will not be available until some time after their graduation, when they start to get access to the job market.

Case study 3

Project: workplace basic education project for low-schooled factory workers who are at risk of unemployment.

Starting date: 1997.

Organisation in charge: Duracell Battery Company (plus Vigon and Bosch), Adult Basic Education Centre, Hageland.

Location: Aarschot.

A partnership between the private and public sectors for a new approach to retraining has raised levels of skills, motivation and work opportunities for hundreds of workers who would otherwise have faced redundancy.

Overview

Jobs for people who have few skills or who are low schooled (low educational attainment) are rapidly disappearing at the Duracell battery plant at Aarschot. The company was bought out in 1995 by the multi-national giant Gillette which began a five-year programme of global reorganisation and re-structuring. New automated machinery is being phased in following a decision to standardise production of batteries world-wide. The majority of low-skill workers at the Aarschot plant will be made redundant unless they can retrain for the high-skill jobs which the new production systems will require. The effect on the local community is potentially devastating. There will be considerable demand for workers with new skills which the present workforce lacks.

Down-sizing and lay-offs or relocation to an area where people have the skills are the usual response in many companies in the private sector. Duracell teamed up with two other companies in the area, Vigon and Bosch, and developed a training programme, which is a "preventive measure", specifically designed to prevent this target group slipping into exclusion. In the past, some plant employees had taken regular adult basic education courses, but they had difficulties in following normal course schedules due to their shift work and family responsibilities.

Menial work which was to disappear first had been done largely by women. Previously, company training was targeted at skilled workers and those at management level. Little training has ever been provided to this group of low-skilled factory employees.

Duracell Aarschot employs 1 100 people, virtually all hired locally. It is a huge company with a turnover of BF 14 billion in 1997 of which approximately BF 10 million were spent on training projects.

Projects

This was a ten-week course of four hours each week. The curriculum was intensive and included basic skills in numeracy and workplace literacy, professional and social skills, quality control, personal computing, communications, problem solving and teamwork. Threatened workers required more than just technological skills to avoid being made redundant. Courses were tailored to meet their specific needs and to help them acquire a very different general approach to the work. New working practices meant they had to be able to adapt to changes at very short notice and work independently, rather than constantly being told what to do. Most lacked the essential learning skills usually gained during the upper school years; programmes had therefore to be designed which would help them learn to learn.

65

Programmes were developed jointly between the human resources departments and the Hageland Adult Basic Education Centre. The centre also provided its teachers. Fabrimetal, the employers' organisation for the sector in the region, was the co-ordinating body for a special fund provided, approved with the union through collective bargaining. The government paid staff for time off to study.

The company's human resources department received applications and then selected the candidates. It also made sure of the staffing levels of the respective divisions but replacements could not always be arranged. Typically, employees worked a shift between 6:00 and 14:00, then went to the class (2-hour session), or conversely they went to the class for two hours and started their shift between 14:00 and 22:00.

Outcomes

Three groups completed the course in 1997 and a further 12 women aged 27 to 43 were starting their training programmes at the time of the OECD visit in 1998. The visit focused on the work at Duracell, although there were also four workers from Bosch. As with many such schemes, employees (all of them women) had families and they therefore found some difficulty in organising work and study around home duties.

The results are a considerable success story: workers who had retrained reported greater enthusiasm and self-motivation, improved work opportunities and increased flexibility and mobility around the factory. A comment often made was that staff were able to do their jobs with much greater insight and understanding; they said they could also work better as a team after the training. At the company level too, the co-operation among management in the three firms had led to improved performance all round.

The workers also commented that as a result of the retraining and introduction to the adult basic education centre, they were committed to continuing in future learning activities. Given the speed of re-organisation and re-structuring and the general family and work commitments, it is not clear yet whether this type of initiative will serve as anything other that a one-off programme for short-term goals or whether it can make a difference to workers whose initial education was at such a low starting point.

The main problems arising stemmed from the heterogeneity of the group. The only selection criteria was one of educational attainment, to determine who joined each group at the start of training. The adult basic education centre in future wants to be able to screen candidates more closely on their numeracy skills; the trainees want a fuller introduction to basic computing, but it is not certain whether the company considers any of this to be a long-term priority.

Case study 4

Project: multi-media and computer training for long-term unemployed, migrants, people with physical disabilities.

Starting date: 1987.

Organisation in charge: Protheus (not-for-profit organisation).

Location: Kortrijk (French border).

Unemployed people with multiple disadvantages and little chance of work had their lives transformed by a carefully-tailored counselling and coaching project aimed at equipping them for new high-technology jobs.

Overview

Kortrijk in West Flanders is on the French border and is a hub of the new technology industry in both countries. This emerging industry has created considerable employment opportunities for people with the required skills and aptitudes. In such circumstances, the disadvantaged, disabled, and low-schooled are highly vulnerable to social exclusion.

In this context, programmes, such as the ones at Protheus, a not-for-profit training organisation, have been created in close partnership with industry on both sides of the border to meet the needs of potentially excluded groups.

Projects

Protheus started to provide training for the long-term unemployed, low-schooled, migrants and people with physical disabilities in 1987. It was called the *Kelchtermans-projecten* after the Minister of Labour at the time and was created to fill a gap in the government's training programmes during a period of very high unemployment. It now has 60 people on courses ranging from training for office workers (its main programme) to graphic design and multimedia work. The latter, multimedia training, is a showcase for Protheus to demonstrate the quality and prestige of the high technology work opportunities for the target groups. The typical training schedule includes 10 months training and two months work experience in industry.

Since 1992, a fully-fledged coaching method has been introduced which covers all different training phases from orientation, training and job search to on-the-job support during the first six months of employment. By using the new coaching methods and keeping up with the latest technological developments, Protheus aims to ensure that all its trainees are productive from day one of employment. The coaching is linked to very close contacts with companies operating in the regional labour market. Trainees are given thorough training in procedures for applying for jobs and briefings from (and detailed interviews with) prospective employers. The course includes unpaid on-the-job work experience with a range of employers; this fieldwork is used as both a recruiting ground for the employers and a means for trainees to assess their own suitability for different jobs.

There are no set criteria for the selection of trainees who are often accepted regardless of their low educational attainment or disabilities. The most important attributes Protheus staff seek is open-minded attitudes to new technological ideas and a clear aptitude for logical thinking and creativity. These are priorities above any questions of prior educational attainment, particularly when being considered for multimedia training. New trainees go through a week-long selection period, during which time their aptitude is determined. The training as much as the industry itself is a multi-national affair. Links have been established with Lille, a French border city.

The EU Social Fund programme called Horizon, the Flemish government (Department of Labour), and the Province of West-Flanders are the main sources of funds. Partnership involves local industries in Belgium and French Protheus is eagerly pursuing inter-European partnerships looking to countries such as Romania.

Outcomes

Seven out of ten Protheus multi-media programme graduates found work in what is a highly competitive field. Two other graduates from the course now work for the organisation as instructors. Both are physically disabled but had little educational disadvantage as they had post-secondary educational experience.

By concentrating on aptitude rather than prior educational achievement, the project opened up new training and subsequent employment opportunities for those participants who would not conventionally have been considered promising candidates for this type of high-tech training.

Innovation and effectiveness

Several issues stand out in the Belgium case studies:

- innovative, extensive and personalised coaching and counselling methods led to notable outcomes, including the recruitment and retention of learners and workers with high level of motivation and peer support;
- a single solution to the social problems of long-term unemployment among working-age women was found in the ISIS project where home-care solution for the seniors was used to generate waged jobs;

- effective partnership of industry, education and government secured funds for training which could transform the working lives of once low-skill workers and could save a community threatened by the changing local economy.

Commentary

The Flemish case studies illustrate most clearly how adult education is only one aspect to consider when attempting to combat social exclusion. Institutions play a role but as one of many partners in a wider network of adult learning and social and economic support. The broad solution is in a range of partners working to clearly defined goals. Without this, as some of the work illustrates, the gains cannot be sustained in the longer term.

Learners repeatedly mentioned the challenge of juggling work, study and family responsibilities; the challenge in the Flemish Community is much greater for women than it is for men, as recognised in many other countries. The ISIS type of flexible work is one of the responses to this challenge. The more complete solution might be in exploring a collective or community-wide solution, rather than tackling individual problems. At the moment, learning, family and work are in large part segmented activities for each individual to reconcile. Integration is needed, with whole families being educated about the benefits of the projects, not just the person who chooses to do the learning and work. Family resistance is too often a reason why women drop out, not only from the work but lifelong learning. There are not a lot of community-based learning initiatives going on in Flanders; even the best of partnership projects are aimed at improving individual employment prospects or specific skills before addressing the needs of the community.

As the case studies clearly illustrate, learning throughout adult life is becoming a necessity rather than luxury or leisure, particularly with the rise of the new technologies (case studies No. 3 and 4) and the changing society and labour market (case study No. 1). Responses need to be unconventional and show more flexibility.

The projects have resulted in creating new routes to employment, improving personal security, raising self-esteem and building a sense of independence. In the case of the ISIS projects, the gains came out of adversity: facing up to the consequences of social decay and the decline of the traditional family. The work was as much a response to the needs of a vulnerable section of society – the elderly – as it was to those of specific vulnerable groups in danger of exclusion from the workplace. It may be a low-cost low-pay solution, but the women who took the jobs did not feel as if they were in a low-pay trap; rather, they saw their career options widening.

The second ethnic minority case study illustrates the fate of a one-shot project: an innovative idea of combining work and study with an important cultural bridging component which did not survive. While its passing is to be regretted, it reflects the emphasis by policy makers that these special initiatives should be experimental and not generalised. The view is now that migrant people should be coached in the regular higher education sector. The project team recognised the importance of addressing not just the needs of ethnic minorities but also of changing the culture of the host country, to be more understanding and accepting.

The retraining of people with low skills and education at the Aarschot Duracell plant is a model experiment of how a partnership, widely supported, can rescue a workforce from redundancy, raise their motivation and enthusiasm, and improve the performance of the company. However, the long-term effectiveness of the project as a "preventive" measure is yet to be seen. As case study No. 4 illustrates, the driving force behind the success of trainees is the ability of staff to identify their aptitudes for the high-tech industry and the quality of the fully-fledged coaching and counselling programme they were able to provide.

Common features of successes in all the projects were new forms of coaching and orientation. Three of the four Belgium projects visited by the OECD were involved in developing advanced coaching which offered more extensive long-term help than most traditional counselling and guidance schemes.

MEXICO

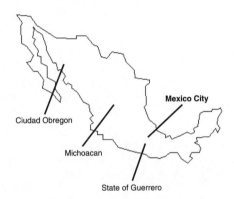

Total population (1996): 96 582 000
– age structure of population 15-64
  (1995): 59.1%;
– age structure of population 65 and over
  (1995): 4.8%.

Land size area: 1 973 000 sq km.

Per capita GDP (1996 prices): US$3 411.

Annual percentage growth rate (1997): 7.0%.

1996 unemployment rate: 5.7%
– proportion unemployed for 12 months or
  more: 2.3%.

Expenditure on education per student (1995): US$1 464.

Percentage of population aged 25-64 with at least upper secondary education:
No OECD data.

Sources: OECD (1998*h*), *Employment Outlook*;
"OECD in Figures – 1998"; OECD (1998*g*),
Education at a Glance.

"If I were not here, I would be at home watching soap operas on TV all day."

The telling response of a middle-aged woman in a remote and impoverished community when asked how she had benefited from Las Misiones' dress making course.

Mexico

Context

Mexico is a vast country of almost 2 million sq. kilometres on the southern extremity of North America, bounded to the south by Guatemala and Belize and lying between the Pacific Ocean and the Caribbean. The sheer size brings considerable geographical and cultural diversity; North and South are like two distinctive countries.

The population of the country is predicted to reach 100 million by the year 2000. Indeed, the population growth in Mexico over the past few decades has been remarkable. When the revolution began in 1910 there were 15 million people in the country. Now, the capital, Mexico City, has a population of over 17 million and is the largest megalopolis in the world. Despite the over-crowded capital, more than a quarter of the country's population still lives in localities each with fewer than 2 500 inhabitants. According to the most recent census, there were about 5.5 million indigenous people in the country in 1995, a minority of whom (14.7 per cent) spoke only native languages.

Just over a third of the inhabitants are below 15 years of age. The proportion of this group of the population is much higher than other countries participating in the study (less than 20 per cent). In Mexico, the sheer number of this young group is posing tremendous demands on the government to meet their needs for education, health and welfare.

The bulging population has affected many aspects of the country's development since the turn of the century. Mexico has been unable to provide satisfactory work for all its inhabitants and parts of the country have been blighted by emigration to the US and by internal migration to the cities. The scale of emigration to the United States is hardly surprising given the economic strength of the US and the fact that the two countries share a 2 000 mile border. In 1994, it was estimated that there were 34 migrants for every 10 000 of population. By region, more migrants are from western states such as Michoacán, Jalisco and Guanajuato, than from other regions. A recent study indicated that there were about 7 million people in 1996 in the US

OECD 1999

who were born in Mexico. Their average age was 20 years and they included about 2 million undocumented Mexicans.

Mexico has been involved in the process of economic globalisation since the early 1980s but this transformation has not benefited a large section of the population. Rich in natural resources, the country was poised to move in the early 1980s from the ranks of developing nations into the role of a modern player on the world stage. But those hopes have been delayed by a series of major upheavals, including a devastating earthquake in Mexico City in 1985; an uprising in the Chiapas state in 1994 which was followed by a wave of political assassinations; and a sharp recession the following year, the effects of which are still being felt.

An export-led recovery began towards the end of 1996 and the economy grew by 10 per cent in both 1996 and 1997 (OECD, 1998c). Despite this growth, Mexico's per capita income is at just US$3 411 in 1996. Also, polarisation of income distribution among Mexican is increasingly posing a challenge. According to the UNDP's 1997 Report on Human Development, the earnings of the top 20 per cent are 13.48 greater than those of the bottom (20 per cent). With the vastness of its land and its huge population relative to the rather limited infrastructure, the informal economy is prevalent: one estimate suggests that up to 80 per cent of the population – 35 million people of working age – is either in the "informal economy" or outside the labour market.

The health status of the population varies markedly in a country that spends just 4.6 per cent of GDP on health. In the relatively wealthy North, indicators such as infant mortality and life expectancy show levels close to OECD averages; whereas the South has health problems characteristic of less developed countries.

Problems of exclusion in Mexico

While Mexico has a wealthy elite and a relatively strong middle class, there are of course those who are poor. Many of them emigrate to the US. The remainder consists of persons working the informal economy, street vendors, housewives, peasants or field labourers. Many survive by selling their artisan wares in the town market or work on large agricultural plantations in the North of the country or in the cities. Mexican adults who are in need of the most basic education are largely in the informal economy and do not form part of the organised labour force

In a market economy such as Mexico's, the inability to purchase goods and services is the principal way of defining social exclusion. One set of statistics (drawn-up on the assumption that the equivalent of two minimum-wage salaries is necessary to purchase the most subsistent basics) indicates that over a third (38.6 per cent) of Mexican households do not reach this standard (INEGI, 1996).

Level of education is another important yardstick of exclusion. According to the 1995 census, 55 per cent of the population aged 15 and over did not get past elementary school; one in five of this group had received virtually no school instruction. The situation is much worse in localities with fewer than 15 000 inhabitants, and for women in general. Not surprisingly, very poor literacy is still a problem for many Mexicans and poses a challenge for adult educators, especially those dealing with indigenous peoples. The most recent census found that 6 million people over 15 years of age were at the lowest levels of literacy. The national average masked huge variations from only 3 per cent in the federal district to 26 per cent in the poorer Chiapas state. The national figure also masked the high average rate of illiteracy of 38.3 per cent among the indigenous people; for this group, in the states of Guerrero, Chiapas and Chihuahua, the figure was more than 50 per cent. Gender differences are important too. In 1995, women recorded poorer literacy rates than did men overall; in the state of Chiapas the women's rate was significantly higher than that for men.

People with low levels of education or with literacy problems have difficulty participating fully in their society, in the democratic political processes and in mainstream economic activities. Poor literacy levels obviously limit their possibilities but equally important, they can reduce the probability of learning in the future: they prevent access to the new technologies which are of increasing importance in the dynamic sectors of the economy.

Rural isolation makes the huge problems of social isolation and exclusion very hard to tackle. The traditional structure of the Mexican family has been altered by the loss of so many people through migration – up to 50 per cent in some rural parts.

Adult learning and social exclusion

A brief history of adult learning in Mexico illustrates just how difficult it is to compensate for inadequate basic education and break down the barriers to inclusion. It raises important questions about how far the country can depend on adult education to combat exclusion and the extent to which other concerns such as health and welfare must be addressed at the same time.

Education has been one of the policy pillars of successive administrations since the overthrow of the thirty-three year old dictatorship through a major revolution (1910-1921). And the approval in 1917 of a new constitution by the newly formed Congress enshrined ideas of social reform, individual guarantees and social justice.

The Secretariat of Public Education (SEP) was set up in 1921 and its first head Jose Vasconcelos began an educational crusade for the people. It tackled the unequal distribution of educational provision throughout the country. In the 1920s, the SEP introduced rural schools as well as cultural missions (see case study No. 2). The proportion of the population on the lowest literacy level was brought down from 80 per cent at the turn of the century to 66 per cent as a result of programmes introduced in the 1920s. However, measures to combat the marginalisation of indigenous localities ended in failure.

A large scale national literacy campaign began in the mid-1940s with the simple objective of teaching adults how to read and write with the help of volunteers and simple materials. But the effort failed because the adults could find no use for the simple reading and writing skills they had acquired within a few months, and so they reverted to illiteracy. In the 1970s, the government took responsibility for adult education and in 1975 the first adult education law established a national system for adult education where literacy and basic education programmes were offered to any Mexican over 15, who had not covered at least nine years of compulsory education.

In 1981, a special institution was created exclusively for adult education, *Instituto Nacional para la Educación de los Adultos* (INEA). It was developed separately from the regular and formal education system which has only a few night classes for young people whose presence is required as part of their employment and who follow the curricula set down for the day pupils. INEA was given responsibility for steering and conducting federal literacy programmes and for co-ordination of efforts by the individual states, the private sector and other social institutions. These programmes are carried out by volunteers who are known as supportive workers (*colaboradores solidarios*). These include about 11 000 graduates of higher education who perform their community service in adult education.

During the eighties, employers were increasingly requiring a basic education school certificate for almost every job and INEA helped fill this void by offering workers the completion of their basic education through open systems of learning. By 1997 it had given more than 1.3 million primary school certificates and 1.24 million lower secondary school certificates. A further 171 000 adult basic education certificates are given each year. But the annual total is still very low compared with the number of children who reach adulthood without having finished basic education.

Main policy approaches

Given the prevalence of poverty, its alleviation is one of the main policy challenges for Mexico. Simply meeting the people's basic needs – food, housing and health care – is a major challenge. The 1995 census showed that almost 7 per cent of homes still had no electricity, 14 per cent had no piped water supply and 26 per cent lacked adequate sewage. The consequences for the health of the inhabitants are devastating, with gastro-intestinal, skin, and respiratory illnesses among the most prevalent of diseases.

Most of the employment policies in place in Mexico are irrelevant to the excluded, since their educational attainment is less than the primary school completion level. Without a lower secondary level certificate, the excluded are out of the mainstream labour market where employment policies generally define their boundaries. Most of the excluded are either in the informal economy or categorised as economically-inactive population.

The *Plan Nacional de Desarrollo* 1995-2000 (National Development Plan) set down the present government's salient policies in terms of education, health, labour, culture and the economy. It proposed a series of strategies that should be adopted by every institution. In terms of educational development, it highlighted the need to pay particular attention to women, indigenous people, peasants, old people, the young, and the unemployed. It also emphasised the need to promote and facilitate co-operation between government and non-government institutions and to improve the situation of the excluded.

Against such a background, adult education plays a variety of roles. It spreads literacy which is particularly important in a country where up to recently many children left school without completing primary education. Apart from aiding individuals to achieve economic goals, higher literacy levels are associated also with health care and empowerment of the excluded. Adult education acts also as a cohesive force in keeping communities together in many rural areas and this can be shown in the case studies in this report.

To these ends, approaches to adult learning have been reassessed. The INEA approach will continue to play a major role but, by the early 1990s, its limitations were becoming more obvious. A policy of providing the same curriculum to women, men, farmers, young and mature adults was not working. The curriculum was seen to be increasingly out of date and out of touch with the needs of adults, especially older people. Little account was taken of the skills they required in order to survive. The reforms, however, do not end the tried and trusted INEA approach to basic education, they introduce new options. More attention is being paid to older adults' needs: there is a greatly expanded set of options to earn a basic education certificate; the curriculum will be modular; credits will be given for previous schooling or vocational achievements. INEA itself is taking a more decentralised approach in response to concerns that it was too "top-down" in the way it operated.

Individual states approach adult education in a variety of ways, ranging from Basic Education Centres that generally have a more formal course approach to some others that use non-formal education techniques. Non-governmental organisations and community groups have rich experience in less formal adult education approaches to help combat exclusion. Many adult educators are trained by CREFAL, which is an autonomous international organisation based in Pátzcuaro. With over 40 years of history, CREFAL uses innovative techniques in adult learning, serving not just Mexico but other Latin American states.

The sheer scale of exclusion in Mexico coupled with limited resources poses a considerable challenge. The difficulties facing providers of formal adult learning are compounded by the dispersal of people over a wide area. It is important to utilise more effectively the informal, community based programmes.

Case studies

Case study 1

Project: community banks for urban shanty town dwellers and rural communities.

Starting date: varies mid-1990s to more recent.

Organisation in charge (service provider): Fundación de Apoyo Infantil (FAI) – not-for-profit organisation.

Location: Ciudad Obregon, State of Sonora.

More than 500 women with little education and few basic skills who live in urban shanty towns or rural communities have seen their families' lives transformed by the introduction of communal banks. The co-operative-run banks are financial mechanism for their micro business activities. Furthermore, the banks are a source of mutual learning and a catalyst for social and economic change.

Overview

The state of Sonora borders the United States, attracting many Mexicans to cross over to the land often portrayed as one of opportunity and hope. There are, however, opportunities in Sonora as well. It is a rich state that contributes significantly to the Gross National Product. Health and education provision are better than in many other states. Cuidad Obregon, one of the largest urban centres with a population of 410 000, is bustling with its maquilador and other export-related businesses in addition to its traditional agri-business. Despite its prosperity, there are considerable numbers of people struggling for survival in the suburban zones or rural areas. Thousands of migrants from rural areas, hoping for work, settle in shanties on undeveloped urban land, with no running water or electricity and where government services are only just beginning to reach.

The Fundación De Apoyo Infantil-Sonora (Children Support Foundation or FAI) is a Non-Governmental Organisation (NGO) which has developed a variety of programmes to improve the conditions of children and their families. It has a director, 28 full-time staff in its headquarters just outside Ciudad Obregon and has a variety

78

of projects around the state. The FAI-Sonora's main focus is women and children, partly in recognition of the fact that women are often left with the difficulties of raising families because their husbands have either crossed the US border or migrated to other parts of the country for work.

The FAI helps women and families in a variety of ways, such as providing a low-cost day care centre which allows mothers time off child-rearing responsibilities to work outside the home; a wide range of programmes targeted to children; a home agricultural production project which is aimed at improving family health and nutrition through organic farming methods and low cost housing using the basic straw and mud materials.

Innovations of FAI-Sonora include the successful development of small community banks into which local people, mostly women, contribute savings and from which they draw to fund their micro-businesses. The women live in rural areas or shanties without commercial banks. Even if there were commercial banks, they would not be interested in financing the women's micro-businesses which are operated mostly in the informal economy. Therefore the women operate their own financial mechanism run on co-operative principles. The Mexican experience has show that men often do not readily acquire money management skills whereas women, who usually have low levels of education, gain the skills more readily and, equally important, find increased self-confidence from involvement in a project. This, in turn, has many benefits for their families.

Projects

Typically, a bank starts with the FAI going into a community and asking a group of interested women to come up with savings of 100 pesos (US$9) each. After three months, the FAI returns to help the women set up the bank, at which point the women themselves, under guidance, draw up working rules and regulations for their branch.

By mid-1998, some 22 communal banks had been established with a total of 550 members. The work is supported by various funding organisations such as the W.K. Kellogg Foundation. In the first four years of operation, the equivalent of US$187 500 had been invested and there were virtually no defaulters on loans. The banks are made up of between ten and 35 members each and the loan and repayment cycle is over four months. Loans are solely for the women's business purposes and the banks' ground rule is that if one member fails on repayment, other members are unable to take a new loan. Members are obliged to reinvest at least a third of their loan in the bank; this money is used to fund other loans or for productive activities of the group.

While the banks are useful sources of investment, they are also the focus for a wide range of learning activities. Communal banks have manuals, such as Basic

Principals of Accounting, which are used as practical teaching materials for reading and writing. Each bank conducts training sessions, depending on requests from and needs of the members. In addition to basic skills, lessons are given on everything from child rearing to health and nutrition. Regular regional meetings are held once a year for members to discuss problems and examples and learn from one another. They also learn how to make presentations to larger groups. The branch management structure too is a source of learning and confidence building: each bank has elections to the board of directors every four months. The short tenure helps everyone to gain leadership skills.

Business skills, including literacy, gained in the process are crucial to the women's success in their micro business operation which is a vital source of family income. The principal products made by the women include: bread; palm baskets; small rugs; preserved fruits and vegetables; bags; small purses; stuffed toys; small arts and crafts. Others buy and sell shoes, cheeses, or cosmetic items or run small shops. The profits are generally small, particularly for women in remote rural areas where there may not be a great demand for their products and from where it is difficult to travel to sell craft and other work at festivals.

Outcomes

More than 2 000 people have benefited from the work of the 550 women involved in the project. The confidence that this participation gives helps build the women's self-esteem. It awakens interest in learning generally and is of direct benefit when it comes to their children. In the words of one woman: "What I have acquired through the bank is self-confidence which is far more than whatever economic gains I have achieved." Another woman commented: "In our group, there is a lot of learning there; we have learned to know ourselves and little by little we have learned how to work together as a group." The concept of working collectively in this way is still relatively new in the area but the skills acquired by women in the communal banks are useful other than for immediate financial gain. The women learn how to prepare and run meetings of the bank and they achieve a sense of social solidarity that benefits the community. This solidarity is reinforced through democratic decision making.

Lives of individuals have been transformed: the elected treasurer of one branch spoke of the isolation she had felt previously when she remained at home and of how her involvement in the bank had helped her self-esteem. Another woman from a rural area who had moved to the city spoke of being very shy, even ashamed of herself, but of now being "much more open", while a third woman who bought shoes in bulk and sold them at a small profit locally said with obvious pride "everybody knows me around here". A fourth woman had been saving to buy a small vehicle but the family decided instead to use the extra money to build two new rooms onto the family home

Formal and informal learning is integrated in the project, combining the non-threatening atmosphere of community-based learning and development with the essential expertise, contacts, knowledge and resources that institutional support brings. This, combined with the continued support with a light touch from the FAI as the banks grow and operate independently, goes a long way to explaining why there are so few defaulters on loans or drop-outs from the development and learning programmes.

Challenges identified by the FAI include the lack of commercial opportunities open to many of the products women make, particularly in the rural areas where demand is low, and the poor employment prospects outside the project; few women have the general education (or certificates) needed for employment, public transport is poor and family responsibilities without the spouses present are considerable. As to FAI itself, like many NGOs, there is always a danger that limited resources could be spread too thin in order to meet so many pressing and different needs: fund-raising for its programmes has recently been taking up more and more of its time and effort due to cut backs in many funding agencies.

Case study 2

Project: Las Misiones Culturales.

Starting date: 1923.

Organisation in charge: Guerrero State Government.

Location: Rural area of Poliutla, State of Guerrero.

An initiative by Guerrero State Government to improve the lives of some of the poorest people in rural Mexico has been long-lasting yet it still sustains high levels of innovation. Success is due in large part to its impressive flexibility in tackling local issues, using the host communities. Government-backed learning programmes are also tailored to help each community generate income and become self-sufficient.

Overview

Guerrero is in the south of the country and is among the five poorest states in Mexico. The number of people who have finished their basic education and become literate is among the lowest in the country, as are the number of families with running water, medical services, and adequate housing. The possibilities for improving the means of production or of acquiring employment are limited. Guerrero has important

81

economic centres such as the tourist resort of Acapulco and the old silver mining community of Taxco. However, it also has zones where – because of geography and resources – it is very difficult to find work or to improve land production methods. The remoteness of certain communities makes it difficult for some to obtain health and education services. Its diversity is not only geographic and economic but also cultural as there are many different indigenous groups in the state.

Poliutla is a typical rural area within Guerrero: half the men and one-fifth of the women have left for work in the United States or wealthier parts of Mexico. There is strong adherence to traditional and conservative life and to the extended family. Such households are among the better-off since men send money home, but employment opportunities are scarce and many homes consist of only women and children.

Efforts to improve the livelihood of communities date back almost 80 years. In 1921, in the wake of the Mexican Revolution, the Department of Public Education (*Secretaria de Educacion Publicia*) established mechanisms for the planning and expansion of the education system. From this effort came the first teachers (*Maestros Misioneros*) who visited the rural and indigenous communities, made reports from each visit, and recruited young people to work as teachers. With the foundation of *Las Misiones Culturales* two years later, came the Mexican Rural School (*Escuela Rural Mexicana*) which supported innovative ideas for the development of competence in individuals and groups. During the first years of existence, *Las Misiones* had a direct influence over the teachers and the training centres (*Centros Formadores de Maestros*). Little by little the work was directed to influence the communities more and the teachers less. *Las Misiones* adopted a special work model whereby various specialists collaborated to furnish knowledge in support of learning programmes. Today, the experts who form a task force are drawn from fields such as masonry, carpentry, music, recreation, handicrafts, basic education, library science, agronomy and health.

Task forces continue to function in eight states, which have sought to transform their policies in order to adapt themselves to the demands of each stage in their history. However, with the current process of decentralisation, each state functions in a distinct manner, giving varying degrees of support to *Las Misiones*. Although insufficient, the resources received up to now have allowed *Las Misiones* to survive and to generate important proposals for community development.

Projects

The Poliutla mission in the Tierra Caliente region is one of twelve in the state of Guerrero, supported by the State Ministry of Education. Typically one supervisor and nine teachers form a mission. When this team goes into a host community, one of the first actions is to carry out a diagnostic investigation of the region, identifying the community's specific development needs such as running water and improved housing. They then go on to identify the local people's learning needs. Courses are developed then promoted, individually, through house visits or by word or mouth. After this, the team runs programmes of education, training and development to meet the needs of individuals and the community. The commitment of the host community is required throughout, which includes housing the team and providing buildings for training courses. The mission team lives and works within the community throughout the life of the project. After two or, at most, three years of aiding a community, the team transfers to another area, but teams will stay longer at the request of the community. The Tierra Caliente project had been going for five years.

Poliutla has a population of 5 000, of whom 232 are students in the project. There are courses such as dressmaking, nursing, music, dancing, carpentry, bricklaying and each course has about 30 students. The courses are run over a normal school year from September to June but hours of instruction are modified in order to accommodate adult students' family and other household responsibilities. Strenuous efforts are made to ensure that the adult students do not drop out during the training. Half the participants are women and the age of the students ranges from 16 to 25 years. Courses are free and focus on "trade as a source of income" rather than academic learning. The completion rate is around 60 per cent but many leave for unrelated reasons such as marriage or work opportunities.

Apart from the training programmes the construction of houses is undertaken as are activities aimed at improving farming techniques. Leadership is the key to the success of a mission: a good leader not only has to merge the ten or more individual teachers with a variety of expertise into a cohesive unit but also has to negotiate with the community leaders in order to generate the working conditions necessary for the installation and effective functioning of *Las Misiones*.

Outcomes

The award of a diploma is recognised by the state as an inducement to many of the participants to remain in the training programmes. Some people are less concerned about certification and more interested in the direct personal benefits to themselves or their families. The area has been hit by the migration of people to larger cities or to the US. Now, many of them, at least, have the basis of a trade they can build on while others develop their musical talents or dancing skills to make a living from Acapulco or other tourist areas. Many women learn dressmaking which they can put to use for their families or to sell clothes to neighbours. Men learn trades, such as carpentry or masonry, that they can use if they stay locally or if they migrate. For many people, the processes of informal education have been the only option to obtain knowledge, permitting them to continue learning, improve their livelihood, or transform their style and habits of working. Often this process of informal education is the only chance a group has for interaction, dialogue and recreation.

Due to *Las Misiones Culturales*, the community now has running water and the once over-exploited forests are being renewed by the community. The team acts as a catalyst, harnessing energies and ambitions in a concerted effort to develop the whole community. The community has also made a commitment to work together, for example raising school funds through the sale of products and doing outside contract work. Equally important is the emergence of teachers eager to take on the tasks of adult education, many of them former students on the project. Quite a few graduates of the project have already become teachers and they say it helps to draw on their earlier experiences.

The project is unusual in that it is community-centred and learner-centred, developing community and learning needs as a whole, rather than focusing on individuals in isolation. Learning becomes very flexible. There is also strong evidence that the combination of learning to acquire trade skills and the development of literacy (usually related to the trades) has helped foster a greater sense of self-reliance within individuals and the community as a whole.

One of the challenges for the mission is to put a time limit on its involvement in each locality. This has been a topic of some discussion of which Poliutla Mission's five-year stay is one example.

On the one hand, it is said that a time limit is important as otherwise the community will become dependent on the outside help rather than rely in the long run on self-help to tackle and solve its own problems. Also, by transferring from one community to another, the mission has been able to reach previously inaccessible rural areas as there are only limited resources available to the team. On the other hand, an observation has been made that the departure of the mission creates a void in the host community, where any other learning opportunities or materials are scarce. Therefore, if learners are left without any further learning opportunities, their acquired skills and knowledge through the mission will be likely to stagnate or regress over the period of time.

Case study 3

Project: indigenous people's own community enterprise.

Starting date: 1981.

Organisation in charge: *Aprovechamientos Forestales de la Cumunidad de Nuevo San Juan.*

Location: Nuevo San Juan Parangaricutiro, Michoacan.

A highly original self-help community programme has regenerated an indigenous community which runs and manages its own community services and a sophisticated business enterprise.

Overview

The indigenous people have made a rich contribution to the heritage of their country but a disproportionate number have been left behind in the push to prosperity. Evidence of this is shown particularly in their education and literacy levels which tend to be among the lowest in the country. For instance, more than 50 per cent of the indigenous people in the states of Chiapas, Guerrero and Chihuahua were at the lowest levels of literacy as measured by OECD countries. For indigenous women the figure was more than 60 per cent.

The state Michoacan is located in the western part of Mexico which has high rates of migration to the US. The indigenous community of San Juan Parangaricutiro is in a region where the levels of education and health care services are below the national averages. San Juan was devastated by volcanic eruption almost 40 years earlier, which forced the inhabitants to move and set up a new town, Nuevo San Juan. They needed to rebuild their lives and their town from scratch. The eruption left 18 000 hectares of land covered in lava and unusable for agriculture.

Projects

In 1981, about 30 indigenous people from Nuevo San Juan lobbied the government for help. Outsiders were exploiting the forest and the community was in danger of having its land expropriated because of in-fighting over ownership and questions of mismanagement. A detailed study of the problems by a government commission recommended turning land over to the community. Problems were far more complex than just issues over land rights and the devastating economic situation; a multitude of other problems also needed tackling. After many attempts were made to join forces with other small towns Nuevo San Juan Parangaricutiro, as the new location was known, contacted a wood company with the result that a body for forest utilisation was set up called *Aprovechamientos Forestales de la Comunidad de Nuevo San Juan Parangaricutiro*.

The project is based on the community's shared values such as communal organisation and conservation of its cultural heritage, including their language, Purhepecha. Self-sufficiency for the whole community is seen as the ultimate objective. The enterprise is divided into two broad sections: business activities (sawmill/forestry, industrial/wood processing, sales) and community services (community transportation system, community stores, programmes for children – sports, environmental education, etc.) Main products include chips, solid wood furniture, milled wood, small pieces of wood and resin for the basis of chewing gum.

Almost all employees or the descendants of the original group are joint owners, with some outside experts also involved. Continuous on-the-job training is provided, with each division determining its own training needs. Scholarships are provided to help people continue their learning. The enterprise has developed an innovative way of complementing modern technology and scientific knowledge. Those with this expertise work in areas such as pest control, side by side with those who have the indigenous knowledge.

In an innovative approach to the management of their entire enterprise, the Community Assembly of 1 200 joint owners is the highest decision-making body. Also, a committee know as the "Group of 60" acts as the executive board. From time to time, they conduct studies on specific management issues as needed. The strategy used is to proceed collectively, working with the Community Assembly, generating informal education processes to get information, analysing the possible consequences of making one decision or another. This strategy produced, for example, the possibility of providing a financing mechanism that is independent of the banks.

The effectiveness and viability of the enterprise are in large measure explained by the continuous, informal learning processes that guide the joint owners for their management and operation of the whole enterprise. During that process, learning occurs. They have collectively developed impressive skills to respond to problems with action, answering questions such as: "How do we organise ourselves?" "How do we produce?" "How do we administer?" Knowledge is seen as having sense if it is possible to use it to resolve situations or to improve the daily life of the individual or the community. In the same manner, "to know how to do something" is a synonym for capability, a concept that covers both knowledge and skills as well as values and attitudes such as responsibility, commitment and honesty.

Outcomes

Overall, it is a very sophisticated and successful project which embraces both its business operation and community services. It is more impressive knowing that people's levels of educational attainment are limited; the majority of older generation only attained up to the primary level and up to the junior high among the younger generation. This diversity creates its own dynamic and tensions over decisions such as whether to invest in new chemical equipment or in new machinery for wood cutting, in reforestation or conservation methods. A balance has to be maintained between commercial viability of the project and its value as a project for the whole community.

The organisation has created 900 permanent jobs and 500 temporary jobs which is a considerable achievement and of great benefit to a community where there are limited outside employment opportunities. Wages at all levels of work are now double the national average and sales from the business operations in 1996-97 exceeded the equivalent of US$7.5 million. The enterprise had developed its markets internationally so that it escaped the worst effects of the currency crisis of 1994 by switching domestic sales to accelerating exports of their products. Without these jobs, many of the people would have migrated to other cities in Mexico or emigrated to the US. They may still be influenced by American culture but they are not compelled by economic necessity to cross the border into the US. One community manager said: "If there was no communal programme, our people would just work to get a daily minimum wage. Our project provides them with jobs, good income, security, health and community care." Now the young people learn skills at home by working and training alongside experts and these skills can be put to use for a long time.

Learning to take what are often basically commercial decisions in a collective fashion is a slow process. It has led to a shift of focus from individual concerns to those of the community and environment. It gives people a sense of empowerment and control over their own lives and a sense of influencing the collective community. They become active participants and not just spectators in decisions about a variety of issues such as investment in new equipment and buildings; reforestation; pest control; plant production; forest plantations of a commercial calibre; and the protection and development of animals and the wider natural environment.

However, there are still problems over land ownership. Some 14 068 hectares are community owned but there are a further 4 072 individually-owned hectares, some of which are a source of dispute. The community wants to buy the individually owned land but it is a slow and tedious process, not helped by the fact that some of the title documents date back to 1900. There are concerns about loss of cultural heritage, including its indigenous language. US influences on the young returning to the community are seen as having a negative impact. Traditions are changing as women have started to work outside of their home, doing what was seen as men's work. Community leaders also want to see much greater interest shown in continuing education and learning. Despite these unresolved problems it is obvious that the whole collective enterprise and particularly the way it is governed by the general assembly has given a sense of self-sufficiency, identity and pride to an indigenous community.

Innovation and effectiveness

Among the many strengths in the case studies, several issues stand out:

- The creation of parallel services such as banks, where mainstream mechanisms do not exist, has provided viable alternatives for the excluded population. The Nuevo San Juan project demonstrates that collective action based on shared objectives can generate prosperity and self-sufficient enterprises.

– Adult education seems to be effective when it is linked to possibilities of transforming family or community life into an improved condition.

– People are more motivated and take advantage of learning opportunities when literacy, knowledge and skills are linked to their basic needs. With these links also, the policy approaches can then be more systematic.

– Mutual and communal adult education schemes in informal settings with no rigid distinction between teacher and learner have led to some impressive results, leading to a far wider sense of inclusion than just that of economic security.

– When people are given control over their own learning, the sense of ownership empowers them far more than when they are not in control. This helps them overcome exclusion more effectively.

Commentary

Mexico is an immense country on the way to becoming a developed nation. Just meeting basic needs of the people, one third of whom are under 15 years old, is a massive challenge at all levels of government. There are huge numbers of excluded people, most of them outside of the country's mainstream economy. Despite the government's commitment and endeavours, services are only just beginning to reach most of the people and are still too scarce relative to the sheer volume of the problems.

Excluded people must help themselves; economic survival is their primary concern. For this very reason, all the projects aim first and foremost at economic viability. Nuevo San Juan's indigenous enterprise is a marvellous story: it illustrates an extremely high degree of competency and sophistication among people who have created their own prosperous, self-sufficient community enterprise which embraces both the business operation and community services. The communal banks in Sonora sprung up where government services were scarce and regular commercial enterprises non-existent. In both cases, the once excluded people took charge of their projects, with support initially from the government (Nuevo San Juan case) or from the non-governmental organisation (Sonora case). The pride associated with the sense of ownership and accomplishment were high. It was even more impressive given a variety of hardships, such as subsistence living conditions, economic and family circumstances and the limited educational attainment that they had to overcome.

All three projects involve either the entire community (Nuevo San Juan and *Misiones Culturales*) or groups in the community (Sonora communal banks). Thus, their learning programmes to help combat exclusion are communal or group-oriented. This is most clearly illustrated by the indigenous people's unique communal learning; individuals do not act alone, nor are their learning needs catered for in isolation from the community. Even in the case of *Misiones Culturales* where courses offered are targeted at the learning needs of individuals, community-wide projects are undertaken side-by-side.

For many excluded people, learning opportunities are scarce, whether institutionalised or through any other source. Learning resources are also very limited. For these reasons, a range of different types of non-formal and informal learning opportunities fill in the gap. This type of learning has gone further, helping empower the people to alter their own circumstances. As the three case studies show, non-formal learning provides a sense of confidence and ownership and it offers practical tools, such as numeracy, banking, enterprise management, technical knowledge, skills, and specific trades. The adult learning opportunities have had a greater impact on people's lives for not being based on compartmentalised knowledge and skills.

The projects described in the case studies are working well but they are not without limitations and problems. Even if people have learned extremely well through their projects, the lack of opportunities and resources may limit their future development. The shortage of opportunities also presents a major obstacle to those wishing to move into the mainstream labour market. This is especially true for women, many of whom have multiple difficulties as they carry on their family responsibilities single-handed. It was also noted in the case of *Las Misiones Culturales* that time constraints on the life of projects severely restricts learning opportunities for many, even though the time limit is designed to prevent dependency among host communities.

Both the communal banks and Nuevo San Juan cases are interesting examples of the creation of parallel mechanisms, to compensate for the lack of mainstream banks and other such institutions. Now, the relationship between these raises new issues such as the possible conflict between the communal enterprise and the increasingly commercialised approach to the marketing of their products. Future tensions need to be considered; in the case of Nuevo San Juan, between its business operation and community integrity and, in the case of Sonora, between the communal banks and the members' business operation.

The importance of support from the government and other agencies, and for good working relations with them, cannot be overstated. Nuevo San Juan has increased the prosperity of the people and has created jobs. However, it seems to

89

have had little impact on maintaining an indigenous language which is spoken mainly by older people. *Las Misiones Culturales* have a long history of commitment to local communities. They need not only strong leaders and dedicated teachers but also support of the education services; often they suffer from limited resources spread too thinly. It is also true of the communal banks where the NGO, *Fundación de Apoyo Infantil-Sonora* is a catalyst for the project. As with many NGOs, it is struggling for resources. It is meeting more challenges to respond to large and varied community needs. To what extent the Fundación's support will be directed to the development and maintenance of the project in the future is yet to be seen.

NETHERLANDS

Total population (1996): 15 494 000
– age structure of population 15-64
  (1996): 68.3%;
– age structure of population 65 and over
  (1996): 13.3%.

Land size area: 41 000 sq km.

Per capita GDP (1996 prices): US$25 511.

Annual percentage growth rate (1997): 3.3%.

1997 unemployment rate: 5.2%
– proportion unemployed for 12 months or
  more: 49.1%.

**Expenditure on education per student
(1995):** US$4 397.

**Percentage of population aged 25-64 with
at least upper secondary education:** 61%.

Sources: OECD (1998*h*), *Employment Outlook*;
"OECD in Figures – 1998"; OECD (1998*g*),
Education at a Glance.

"*At school you could discuss anything that was worrying you. Women who were having a hard
time at home always found help in working out a solution.*"

A former trainee of a Womens' Vocational Training College.

Netherlands

Context

Many analysts praise the "Dutch Model" of economic recovery. Once at the bottom for economic performance in Europe, the Netherlands is now a prosperous country. Its per capita GDP is the equivalent of around US$25 500, having risen by 3 per cent a year since 1993. The level is 8 per cent higher than the EU average – in 1988 it was 1 per cent below. Although this is still in absolute terms lower than ten other OECD countries, the long-term trend upwards contributes to a positive social climate and a strong consensus on policy issues.

A population of 15.5 million is crowded into a small country of 41 000 sq. kilometres, bordering Belgium, Germany and the North Sea, from which much of the coastal terrain has been reclaimed behind dikes. With 380 people per sq. kilometre, the Netherlands is second only to Korea (465) among OECD countries for density of population. With such a concentration of people, any breakdown in social or political consensus is quickly felt, as it was in the early 1970s when a wage explosion and two dramatic oil-price slumps added to already weak fiscal policies. Severe trade imbalances, under-used labour and production capacity as well as under-performance resulting from economic policies of the early 1970s, created what economists then called the "Dutch disease".

Transition to recovery was slow and painstaking: the government's social policy document for 1998 points to a 15-year process of economic recovery since the early 1980s, following agreements with the social partners for restraint over wage claims, the encouragement of part-time work and a reduction in average working hours. Since 1994, the number of jobs has risen and unemployment has fallen from 8.7 per cent to 5.5 per cent – one of the lowest among OECD members – and is expected to fall to 4.7 per cent in 1999. Long-term unemployment as a proportion of the total out of work has fallen by nearly a quarter. The extent to which hardship if not poverty has been alleviated is shown in the OECD *Employment Outlook* report of June 1998: the Netherlands is one of only six countries where structural unemployment declined through the 1990s and one in only three – the others being the USA and Ireland – where the number of households without anyone in work decreased.

The "Dutch model" that analysts now refer to has to be seen in the context of the depth of the 1970s slump and the nature of the subsequent recovery. The 1998 OECD *Economic Survey* analysis of the Netherlands highlights two areas where the economy is still vulnerable in an otherwise strong recovery: the preponderance of part-time work among the new jobs and the number of people still receiving social security benefits. Two-thirds of the new jobs created have been part-time work; while this has benefited some groups significantly, notably single mothers seeking a return to work, it makes the picture of recovery overall appear somewhat less impressive, although still significantly better than most other European countries. There is also a cultural difference in attitudes, since the Netherlanders take a very positive view of part-time work as "real work" and of there being more to life than the job. A quarter of the labour force is either on social security or job creation schemes which is still well above the level of the early 1980s.

The number of women participating in the labour market has grown dramatically. In 1970, they accounted for just a quarter of the workforce; by 1995 women made up almost a half (47 per cent). This level is about the EU average, though below the levels of Scandinavian countries, with which the Netherlands shares other characteristic of employment and social policy. Much of this work is part-time, in accordance with the statutory right of people to work part-time in the Netherlands, so it is much more common than in most EU countries. However, long-term unemployment rates among women with little formal education are four times higher than those among the unemployed population as a whole and almost twice as high as those for poorly-educated men.

Problems of exclusion in the Netherlands

The government recognises that problems of social exclusion and poverty remain. But in the latest paper on the subject, *The Other Face of the Netherlands*, ministers contend that exclusion is a result of individual circumstances, not collective ones. The paper argues that poverty is not limited to people on minimum incomes, since people on higher incomes or with large debts can experience isolation. It argues also that not all people on minimum incomes are in poverty since some feel that – in the absence of unexpected problems – they are able to live adequately at that level since the minimum wage is 50 per cent of the median salary.

Against the background of economic growth, and continuing expansion of the labour market, the government's approach to social exclusion focuses very heavily on employment, rather than on other dimensions of exclusion. The recent policy paper *Lifelong Learning: the Dutch Initiative*, is distinctive in its heavy emphasis on employability, and on improvements in education to bring adults up to the level of initial schooling, rather than broader notions of cultural or social benefit. It does, however, take a broad definition of employment, giving a strong indication of the important role part-time work plays and recognising the role of voluntary activity in countering exclusion and contributing to the broader health of the community.

Problems arising from exclusion have been identified by the government in three areas: early withdrawal from the labour market, unemployment among immigrant communities, and the widespread belief that women are still under-represented in the labour force despite the growth in employment rates.

In the past, the government had taken a lenient view over disability benefits, which has been used as a way of gracefully easing older and disaffected people out of the workforce, especially during industrial restructuring. As a result, effective retirement age fell, with a growing cost in benefit payments and loss of skills in the labour market. The regulations have since been tightened, and it is now expensive for employers to dispose of employees in this way. However, at present only one in four people aged 55 to 65 are in employment (a low proportion by international standards). Big firms such as the Wavin factory in Hardenberg have been experimenting with strategies to ease the problems of older workers who are locked in jobs with which they are increasingly dissatisfied. By offering transfers to less responsible or part-time jobs – without proportionate loss of income or pension rights – they prevent exclusion among older workers while opening up new opportunities for younger staff. However, such schemes have yet to command public support.

A second factor is unemployment among immigrant communities which in larger cities is up to four times higher than the rates for the rest of the population. Although immigrant groups in general have lower educational levels, this is not universal; there are well qualified people among refugee groups. Problems they face, however, include difficulties learning the Dutch language and obtaining certification of competence acquired in other countries. The situation for those in concentrated migrant communities in the large cities is very different from that of those more thinly dispersed in other towns. The Netherlands has a relatively high proportion of foreign nationals (5.1 per cent of the population) and has a history of tolerance towards immigrants. There were waves of Italian, Moroccan and Turkish arrivals in the 1960s and 1970s. Large Surinam and Antillean communities also live in the Netherlands. Numbers of new immigrants peaked at 60 000 a year before European-wide legislation reduced the flow. By the early 1990s it was down to 37 000.

The third special group is women, especially those who are single. Women have traditionally participated less in the labour market in the Netherlands than in most other European countries. This pattern has now been changed, and participation exceeds the EU average, assisted by very positive policies on part-time employment. However, there are special problems for women with children who have experienced family breakdown. They are able to claim benefit without seeking work until their youngest child is five – a reduction from the former limit of 12 years – but shortage of childcare can make employment difficult, and can create a poverty trap. Childcare is not always free; it depends on which municipality women live in and is related to income.

Adult learning and social exclusion

The 1991 OECD review of national policies for education in the Netherlands pointed to "the profound sense of confusion" in the adult education system. It was strong on "general interest" courses and employer-led training, and the country was waking up to the need to co-ordinate efforts for the unemployed and low-skilled workers. But there was far to go; overlap and duplication, lack of attention to the training needs of the many small employers and the lack of commitment to lifelong learning entitlements all needed urgent attention.

Measures to combat social exclusion in the early 1990s failed to draw on the potential of adult learning beyond using it, as many countries in North Europe were, as a tool for short-term labour-market adjustments. In 1993, efforts to reduce the 1 million adults registered as disabled (and costing 5 per cent of GDP) focused wholly on reassessing individuals and redefining disability. Little effort was made to identify education and training initiatives that might assist many registered disabled back into the labour market, even though it was clear that a route back to new types of employment would have been welcomed by many of the excluded.

The Netherlands has been highly successful academically. It is a world leader in higher education, with one in five of the population having completed higher education level education. Its secondary school attainment levels are less outstanding, though still at the OECD average, with six in ten adults having completed upper secondary education. Despite the confusing state of adult learning, the official figures show a healthy level of uptake: in the mid-1980s, one-in-five adults was in regular adult learning programmes, which grew to more than one-in-three a decade later. A large proportion of these, however, were school and college-leavers aged 18 to 25 years – many of whom were on apprenticeships – rather than adults returning to learn.

The government has concluded that while the adult learning industry was very healthy, it was not serving the most vulnerable groups as effectively as it might. In this, it echoed the warnings in the review of education system in the Netherlands that the large and growing adult education industry was dominated by the private sector and serving disproportionately the interests of the employed and well-educated (see OECD, 1991).

A further distinctive factor has been the strong gender divide in vocational training, with programmes in technical areas almost exclusively male, and health care and education almost exclusively female. This has been mirrored in the labour market, where women have traditionally been employed in specific areas, and where women's participation has been generally low. A range of initiatives has been undertaken to rectify these features, including financial weightings to institutions which recruit women onto non-traditional programmes, and the movement of Women's Vocational Training Centres.

Main policy approaches

The Adult and Vocational Education Act currently being implemented, addresses these issues and brings all public sector post-school education except for higher education into a single structure, the Regional Centres of Education (ROCs). There are 46 ROCs, mainly very large multi-site institutions, some of them with as many as 25 000 students. Some specialise in high skills fields, but most offer a broad range of provision. Typically three quarters of their students are young people on vocational education programmes, with the balance divided between adult vocational work, basic education, evening classes and general education for young people. All students pay a fixed contribution (defined by the Ministry) and fees at levels set by individual Centres. The Act introduced an outcome-based funding system for ROCs, with funding dependent on successful completion of agreed programmes (payment by results), which is due to be fully implemented in the year 2000. The funding scheme will provide weighting for specific categories of learner, including people of foreign origin, young women on technical courses, and a number of other specific target groups.

There is a number of alternative institutions – supported by a range of stakeholders including the trade unions, employers and municipalities – of which the Women's Vocational Training Centres form a notable example, delivering vocational training to specific groups (case study No. 3).

The most notable feature of the Netherlands' approach to unemployment is its very active commitment to the creation of new jobs. The "Melkert Jobs" initiative – named after the former Minister of Employment – aimed at returning unemployed people to the labour market at the minimum wage level through new jobs created in the public sector. Subsidies were given in the short term to employers, in the hope that, by reducing the marginal costs of new employees, the newly-created jobs and the individuals in them would prove to be of value and that posts would become permanent. This initiative has succeeded, no doubt influenced by underlying economic growth, and the general expansion of the labour market. There appears to be less resistance than one might have expected to the idea of actively targeting individual people with the implicit threat of benefit withdrawal for those who do not participate.

97

This approach is backed by devolution to the municipalities of responsibility for tackling unemployment, with considerable discretion over how they use funds to achieve this. There are 600 municipalities, ranging in population from 10 000 to 750 000 people. The 15 largest have drawn up integrated policies on "work, education, safety, care and liveability". Municipalities are responsible for the payment of benefits, and have been given discretion in the deployment of these funds to allow for experiment and for flexible strategies to deal with particular circumstances. An example is the payment to the municipality of the equivalent of US$8 500 from the Ministry of Social Affairs and Employment for every long-term unemployed person who is placed in a job. The municipality has the freedom to use the funds flexibly, including subsidising employers' costs, funding training costs or project work, and paying for initiatives such as Nieuw Werk (case study No. 2).

The initiatives concentrated on those excluded from the labour market, although people interviewed about the general problem, including representatives of the Ministries of Education and of Social Affairs and Employment, recognised the existence of other forms of exclusion. Specific groups identified included the homeless and drug users, for whom adult education was not seen as the primary need, and those retired on state pensions, especially women, who were believed to experience real isolation. Responsibility for this latter group rests primarily with the Ministry of Sport, Welfare and Housing. A series of interventions by government has reversed the upward trend in claims for unemployment, disability benefits, and early retirement.

Case studies

Case study 1

Project: to improve education and job opportunities for ethnic minorities.

Starting date: 1996.

Organisation in charge: De Landstede College, Zwolle.

A unique assertiveness training project for ethnic minority students succeeded in reforming the negative attitudes of employers seeking new staff. The project helped students generate social capital – networks, contacts and confidence – which ethnic majority students take for granted.

Overview

Young people from ethnic minorities are more likely than any other group to drop out of initial education, reject higher education opportunities and suffer discrimination at work. Drop-out rates from vocational college among first and second generation migrants to the Netherlands range from 50 to 70 per cent, compared

98

with 43 per cent for the rest of the student population. A significant problem for minority young people in the labour market is the perception of the young people – by themselves and by the majority population – as victims seeking help, rather than as individuals seeking to contribute to society and the economy.

Since 1992, the government has encouraged the integration of minority groups into a multicultural society; racial discrimination in education and employment is illegal. All those employing more than 30 people must declare the proportion of ethnic minority employees, indicating the level of jobs held.

Each region has a target, based on the proportion of minority people in the local population. In Zwolle, the target is 3.5 per cent, but the actual level reached is nearer 1 per cent. Hidden discrimination on the basis of names is common at the earliest stages of recruitment; many minority applicants are, therefore, never invited for interviews. Selection tests with cultural bias are also alleged.

Some employers are gradually changing their views; retailing for example is a trade where they see minorities as a new market and are seeking to recruit staff from these groups; one national supermarket chain has designed a uniform specifically for Muslim women employees. A team in Zwolle is working on a project to boost participation by groups of foreign origin in education and to change public images of minority young people. A lack of awareness among the general population, rather than prejudice, was seen by the team as the greater barrier to inclusion. There were two key reasons for the change in employers attitudes: on the one hand they did not want to appear prejudiced; on the other, they knew they had no alternative sources of recruitment as the country was reaching a state of full employment.

Projects

The PAJO project was initiated by De Landstede College in Zwolle in 1996 in co-operation with FORUM, the National Institute for Multi-cultural Development. De Landstede is the smaller of two post-secondary school Regional Colleges in the area, with 7 000 students on 20 sites. The college has been involved in work of this kind for over 10 years and, under a national scheme, is designated the one within its region to make special provision for "international work". It has 350 students of foreign origin who take an 18-month course of general education and orientation, including Dutch as a second language, leading to a national certificate.

PAJO was first created in Zwolle, but FORUM, the National Institute for Multi-cultural Development (across all areas of public policy including Education, Health, and Welfare) is now seeking to establish similar schemes throughout the Netherlands, with project funds from the Ministry of Education. A video and information packs about the project was produced, and a television programme was planned.

99

The strategy of the project is to empower groups of students from minority communities to work together to find ways of increasing their employment prospects, to sell this image to employers and to develop the sort of informal networks of support and contacts which other young people already have. Students are encouraged to think positively about their skills and resources, and to respond assertively to promote a strong self image.

The choice of a law student from Turkey as a project leader was made so as to create a role model for the team. Successful past students are encouraged to keep in touch with the team. Team members are provided with personal business cards, and have access to telephone facilities at the college for communicating with employers.

All students follow the mainstream curriculum of the College; in addition the "team" meets fortnightly so that members can be provided with individual support and training in communication skills, assertiveness and teamwork by their teacher and the project leader. The team consists of 25 students, from a very wide range of ethnic backgrounds (Turkey, Somalia, Surinam, India) and includes some Dutch students who wish to take an active part in promoting opportunities for their minority colleagues. The meetings are also used for the planning of initiatives, which involve approaching individual employers to make presentations and engage in discussion about minority young people.

As the project has become widely known, employers have begun to approach the team directly to ask for presentations. Similar activities have developed in other areas, and a network of students is developing, which has also engaged in Parliamentary lobbying and media briefings. Such high profile activities are reported to have had a significant impact on how images of minority employees are presented in the media.

Students join the team in addition to their normal studies, and the typical student involved in the project is likely also to be in part-time employment for 15 hours a week. The commitment is a substantial one and attendance by some team members is therefore said to be erratic. There is no opportunity for them to acquire credit for this work, although some believe that this should be possible, and it would presumably increase student motivation.

Outcomes

Although employment is not the primary goal of the project, some students have found jobs as a direct result of the work, and a recent approach has persuaded an insurance company to create six jobs for members of minorities. There was also a lower drop-out rate and a better image for the traineeships, attracting others into education.

The project is successful in motivating students to take control of their own lives and employment prospects, and to become active, rather than passive, participants in the labour market; it strengthens their position and sends important signals to employers. By engaging in lobbying activity the team has helped to create positive images of minority employees. The team now represents a centre of expertise in understanding the issues faced by ethnic minorities seeking work, in a context where employers are willing in principle to recruit, but unsure about how to do so. It has created jobs for minority students, and is seen as a model for imitation elsewhere in the Netherlands, for participation by minority groups – including disabled students – in higher education and employment.

The project's success depended partly on the enthusiasm of the key staff; they have helped promote it so well that it has been taken up in other regions of the Netherlands. The staff involved work well beyond the time requirements of their contracts; some students also commit considerable time and energy for no formal reward. Student participation and motivation might be increased if credit was given to the learning which clearly takes place among team members.

One of the critical success factors was the commitment of a highly charismatic leader who ensured that the work of staff went much further than that of basic support, involving them in the learning process and ensuring detailed follow-up of graduates and continued pastoral and professional support in the workplace.

Case study 2

Project: return long-term unemployed, low-skill adults to work.

Starting date: 1996.

Organisation in charge: The Nieuw Werk organisation, founded by the Municipality of Eindhoven, the Employment Agency and the Agency of Temporary Work Start.

Long-term unemployed and refugee adults who had given up all hope of work found unprecedented opportunities through a project that tailored careers guidance and training to suit their circumstances. They were trained for new jobs in high-tech industry.

Overview

Eindhoven is a city with an exceptionally healthy economy, even by Dutch standards, and where employers are anxious to find workers. As a result they are willing to accept them with lower qualifications than in the past. The regional economy is dominated by a handful of multinational electrical firms such as Philips and Daf which devolved many functions to subcontractors during the late 1970s to early

1990s. There is thus a large and thriving high-skills, small to medium enterprise sector, experiencing continued growth in demand. There are 4 000 small companies involved in the region – a quarter of them one-person firms.

The main problem is that the healthy economy and near full employment has left the city with a severe shortage of people available to fill jobs. Nieuw Werk is an organisation founded by the Municipality of Eindhoven, the Employment Agency and the Agency of Temporary Work Start. Nieuw Werk co-ordinates the REGIOMet project, which was launched on the initiative of the Regional Foundation of Companies in the Metal Industries and consists of four interlinking projects. The aim of the first projects was to get 300 long-term unemployed people into work over a three-year period (due to end in 1998). The other three REGIOMet projects are aimed at developing the skills of workers within the metal and electrical industries and at improving the image of this sector.

One project was designed to take individuals from the long-term unemployment register and train them to fill the vacancies for lower-skilled workers in the industry. It was unusual in that it worked from a list of long-term unemployed people in the region provided by the Welfare Agency and the Municipality of Eindhoven. Project staff called them for interview and offered them short training and employment in the industry, despite the fact that the interviewees had no previous interest or experience in this sector. Refusal to take a job meant, however, that the unemployed people faced having their welfare benefit withdrawn.

Projects

More than 1 800 names were provided and the agreed target was to train 300 long-term unemployed (the actual number trained was 460) and put 250 of these into jobs within three years. By mid-1998, 180 had found jobs, and staff estimated that this would rise to about 220 by the end of the year. The register classifies every individual on first enrolment into one of four categories, ranging from those considered employable without further training to those with few prospects of employment. The project was limited to working with those in the two "least employable" categories – including some previously considered unemployable – who had not been actively encouraged to seek work. The average recruit was aged 34 and had been unemployed for four years. More than 50 per cent of participants were of foreign origin – compared with 40 per cent in the local population as a whole – and 63 were women, although the project was working in a traditionally male employment sector. Most recruits had no qualifications or were of low educational attainment. There were, however, some foreign workers (including refugees) with relatively high levels of education but who suffered from discrimination because of employers' lack of familiarity with them (especially in small firms in small communities).

An important element of the programme was the career planning, where individuals were each helped to develop a medium-term action plan. Group training, social skills, and a sufficiently sympathetic but tough training environment were identified as important. So too was the rapid manufacture of visible products by the trainees, strengthening pride in personal achievement and quality from the beginning. Emphasis was also put on the need for trainees to recognise that many long-term unemployed people had good reasons for having not been in work. Respect for individuals was seen as essential if the new workers were to rebuild self confidence. Considerable stress was put on the need to help trainees prepare for the work and to know what was expected of them in the medium term. Each trainee was given a named professional guidance worker to turn to in the event of on-going problems, including domestic and financial ones.

The other projects under REGIOMet were less well developed, but were linked with the project for the long-term unemployed. In one, 600 of the current workforce of the industry were being trained for higher-level tasks; a second project aimed to create a job rotation scheme, whereby existing employees would be freed to undergo training while specially trained unemployed people temporarily filled their posts. This was yet to start in small firms, although one large company had used the scheme for 20 unemployed people, and negotiations were in progress in mid-1998 with another company for a further 60 places. The third project aimed to promote the image of metal and electrical industries, which are widely regarded as offering dirty and unrewarding employment.

The project has four main partners: Nieuw Werk identifies and selects individuals and jobs, and gives support to individuals once they are placed in work; the municipality provides funding and subsidises placements; the Regional Vocational Training Centre offers specifically designed training, and the Regional Foundation of Companies in the Metal Industry provides links with employers to help improve quality in the industry. All four are held in very high regard by employers. The training centre in 1997 trained 1 069 people, on programmes averaging four months. The close working relationship has created opportunities for other kinds of collaboration and project work, and closer networking between firms. Companies are co-operating more, although there is a slow and long-term evolution of collaboration, and of recognition of a common need for training.

Outcomes

The project's success was attributed substantially to the high motivation and positive attitudes to work among the trainees, and to the fact that the training offers a broad range of low-level skills, so workers are trained for a variety of jobs. In an expanding economy, measures to try and identify individuals who might benefit from retraining, regardless of background can work if they are linked to efforts by, employers to identify where new jobs can be created. This was made easier in Eindhoven since the jobs were created at marginal cost: a 50 per cent subsidy came from the municipality. Whether such an approach could work effectively in a less buoyant economic context is unclear; but it is evident that the strategy of negotiating between individuals and employers can get some people into work who would not otherwise have been recruited, and that some new jobs do get created.

Employers now see REGIOMet as a good source of potential employees who are ready for work and who cost relatively little during an initial trial period in work. For example, Jos Verhees has 17 employees using computer controlled machines to produce small metal components for 60 customers in the car industry, medicine and agricultural firms. His company was having problems meeting the expanding demand and was suffering from a shortage of labour; he was therefore pleased to be approached by REGIOMet and by mid-1998 had three employees recruited through the programme. The owner, manager and his deputy agreed that the recruits were valuable, despite relatively low skill levels, since they could be trained on the job more quickly than young recruits from vocational training schools (who typically take two to three years to become fully productive). The initial subsidy was welcome, but the three moved quickly on to permanent contracts; temporary subsidised jobs were being converted into permanent employment growth.

A Bosnian refugee – a former press photographer in his own country – who arrived in the Netherlands in 1995, took two months off-site training and an eight-week placement before joining Jos Verhees on a six month initial contract. He was very pleased with the job, despite having had no previous interest in engineering. His permit to stay had been extended to 2002, and he intended to apply for Dutch nationality. His main criticism of the scheme was that it grouped together refugees, some of whom had considerable formal education in their own countries, with long-term unemployed Dutch people, whose needs were different.

Alongside the initiative was the Regional Foundation of Companies in the Metal Industries, a trade association with over 150 members, which aims to improve the quality of the industry, help identify skills shortages and promote training in higher-level skills and in management. This meshes well with the REGIOMet strategy of introducing new labour with basic skills at the bottom, allowing more experienced workers to take on higher-skilled jobs.

The questions which remain about the initiative concern those people who were not recruited onto the programme (the target is only 300 of the 1 800 initially identified). Are the rest experiencing even greater exclusion? There is also an issue about the mixture of people involved in the training. Unlike the Anna Polak School case (case study No. 3) the mix of recruits to REGIOMet is not planned to be diverse, and clearly there are issues such as the problems in training the long-term unemployed alongside recent refugees. A further issue is the continuation of the programme. Nieuw Werk appears to be a success, in securing ongoing employment for long-term unemployed people, and in generating increased economic activity. However, its project funding from the municipality was only for three years, and its future is under question. There are discussions about privatising the organisation, and operating in future as a commercial company.

Case study 3

Project: boosting women's job prospects by removing discrimination.

Starting date: 1996.

Organisation in charge: Anna Polak School in Zaandam.

A project designed to boost women's job prospects and change labour market attitudes to women has had a remarkably high success rate. Colleges involved have gained international acclaim for their work.

Overview

Women were severely under-represented in the Dutch labour market in the 1970s and early 1980s, suffering discrimination in many areas. Substantial numbers of women were experiencing poverty, especially those whose relationships had broken up, leaving them dependent on benefit and unreliable alimony, and with childcare problems which made returning to work difficult. The problems were further compounded for women from ethnic minorities who may have had language and cultural difficulties, despite long periods of residence in the Netherlands. In addition, women are heavily concentrated in vocational areas such as caring and service industries; they represent a very small proportion of workers in technical occupations.

Recent legislation has stressed equality in the labour market, formalised the rights of parents to paid leave, increased the volume of public sector childcare, and imposed regulations requiring equal treatment in general conditions of recruitment and employment.

Vocational training colleges exclusively for women (WVTCs) were created in the early 1980s by the trades unions, concerned about both the under-representation of women in the labour market, and perceptions that the mainstream vocational training colleges – which focused on the training largely of young men for technical craft occupations – were not well adapted to the needs of mature women. The colleges were particularly perceptive in recognising the extent to which learning styles were often different for women than they were for men and that many working environments were hostile to women.

Recruits to the colleges are mainly in the age range of 18 to 50 years, and from 1984 to mid-1998, some 11 000 women were trained, with 80 per cent finding employment afterwards. In some occupations such as financial administration – where older people are generally seen as more reliable – the colleges will admit older women. The most rapid period of growth was experienced by the WVTCs in 1996, when the government changed the benefit regulations, requiring women with children to actively seek work when their youngest child reached 5 years, rather than 12 years as before.

Projects

The Anna Polak School is one of seven WVTCs in the Netherlands. The college aims not only to get women into work but also to modify the behaviour of the labour market in relation to women. It does this through tailored programmes, individual support to trainees throughout – and beyond – their participation in a college programme and through close working relationships with a range of partners. The partners include the vocational training centres and employers, who place high value on the quality and relevance of the Anna Polak School training, on the negotiating of good quality work placements, and on the training for areas where women are likely to be successful and well treated.

Two programmes are offered at the Anna Polak School: "Learn as you Work" and "Learning House". The Learn as you Work programme is a course for women in Purmerend, a small town north east of Amsterdam. Trainees usually complete a one-year programme which combines theory and practice. They learn about the labour market recruitment, how to complete application forms effectively, personal guidance, career choice and managing careers alongside domestic commitments. At the same time, they work in the "company" Anna Polak and Partners, providing business services on a commercial basis, gaining work-related skills. The course does not offer formal accreditation but aims to help broaden horizons with a range of additional programmes such as language training for those who need it.

The Anna Polak School carries out some training in house, but commissions much from the new regional centres for education (ROCs). Staff at the school are, however, very clear about the conditions on which they will do this, and sometimes insist on training ROC staff in ways of working with mature students, especially women. The WVTCs are privately-funded institutions which pride themselves on their independence, flexibility and creativity. There were, at one time, seven such institutions, but two chose to merge with the ROCs. The view at Anna Polak School was that the special mission for women was lost in those institutions which joined the ROCs. While this independent status of those who refused to join means there is a lack of continuous public funding, the Anna Polak School is not concerned about the financial future; staff believe that the quality of its work secures sufficient public and private funding. A growing proportion of its budget comes from employers, who buy training programmes for women employees in specific areas in which Anna Polak specialises, such as information and communication technologies (ICT), or generic programmes for particular groups of women, including the low skilled and those from ethnic minorities.

Unlike other training institutions, the WVTCs also place heavy emphasis on brokering, on seeking new and developing areas of employment and on designing courses to fit specific needs. The graduates gain relevant and specialist skills which give them unique advantage in the labour market by comparison with tradition-ally-trained young people. Examples include: a programme for administrators in the funeral business; the shift of information technology office administration train-ing towards network management; recognising the growing need for such skills in conventional offices; the inclusion of Internet training in all programmes; and the provision of a programme on Website design in response to evidence of growing skill shortages. The Anna Polak School puts particular emphasis on innovation; courses are never run for more than two years without a review, to ensure that the staff and students keep up to date with the latest developments in the labour mar-ket. The WVTCs seek to develop specific skills which enable their graduates to offer some additional or specialised skills, or a broader background. The colleges oper-ate a strong positive discrimination policy, deliberately recruiting ethnically diverse student groups, and with quota policies for students and staff.

Another feature of the curriculum is that all students receive training in key skills, ensuring that their underlying basic skills, including communication, numer-acy and literacy are at least as good as those of their younger competitors in the labour market. The curriculum also puts strong emphasis on individual attention. Students are carefully selected at entry to ensure that they are motivated and understand the difficulties likely to be faced by women (mainly single mothers) returning to study and to the labour market. Throughout the training and work placement, they have access to individual support. The Anna Polak School also actively creates student groups and encourages them to provide mutual support – during the course, during work placement and beyond. In the view of the college staff, it is the group support at a time of considerable change which ensures low drop-out rates among the women. Close attention is given to learning styles and the ways women learn, being often more reflective than men, especially in technical fields.

The links with employers are a vital element of the WVTC formula. The staff carry out continual market research with potential employers, identifying the needs as they emerge, and developing programmes in partnership. Staff consider carefully how "woman friendly" the field of employment is before planning a course, and in selecting work placements. The school withdrew a course in construction skills after graduates had found difficulties in the working environment. Staff plan placements, sometimes arranging for three students to work together in situations where mutual support may be important. They also use networks of former students to identify trends in the labour market, or emerging training needs, and work closely with the trades unions on these issues. The WVCTs also provide specific training for employers. This includes training in ICT for women and more generic training for women with low skills or from minority groups in need of additional support. This work helps maintain a range of income sources, and opens the Anna Polak School and other colleges for use in children's school holidays when the main programmes do not take place and special courses for women, funded by employers, can operate. It also strengthens the networks for intelligence gathering and builds links for identifying possible student placements.

Outcomes

The WVTCs have been identified internationally as a valuable model of adult education. The colleges are involved in a range of transnational EU projects, and are called on to provide consultancy on women's education in other countries. The Anna Polak School in particular recognises that one reason for the success is the healthy state of the labour market, where demand for skilled employees exceeds supply; but the staff also believe they produce work-ready graduates with a greater range of up-to-date and relevant skills than could be obtained elsewhere. Networking has proved to be a key part of the success, which is reflected in the fact that eight out of ten women on the courses gained employment – 60 per cent of them in the firms where they had completed industrial placements.

Innovation and effectiveness

Several factors stand out in the Netherlands case studies:

- – The highly innovative anti-discrimination programme at De Landstede College has found ways of galvanising the efforts of ethnic minorities, to help them take control of their lives and change long-standing negative attitudes among employers.

- – The experience of recruiting non-traditional people, such as ethnic minorities from De Landstede College and women from Anna Polak School in Zaandam, is changing perceptions in the workplace and will probably have lasting benefits for minority groups.

- A sophisticated partnership of public subsidy and private innovation has created lasting jobs – with guaranteed training and wage levels – which are more than schemes to massage unemployment figures.

- The Anna Polak School project created adult learning materials and training methods that were tailored to the needs of an exclusively female audience. A particular strength was the attention to detail in intelligence gathering in order to know precisely the needs of employers and of the skills.

Commentary

It is clear that the scale and impact of these projects is affected both by the overall state of the economy of the Netherlands, and by the specific structures of the labour market in particular places. There is clear evidence that in some areas employers are adjusting their expectations of new recruits, and their attitudes to training because the economy, approaching full employment, leaves them no alternative. Thus one employer said that he would like new well-trained recruits, but recognised that he would not get them, and would be happy to take intelligent well-motivated people, especially refugees with good formal education, and train them on the job. Once established, it seems possible that such workers will provide practical demonstration of their competence and value to the firm, and thus change attitudes. The case studies illustrate, however, that this approach can also succeed in less flourishing economic periods, provided it is supported by intensive coaching, co-operation with companies, a combination of work and learning, supporting the individual with an integrated and tailor-made approach.

Education has an especially important role in assisting those suffering less extreme forms of exclusion, especially those in danger of becoming permanently excluded through low skills and problems with personal relationships which had disrupted their lives. Several of the projects are clearly making an impact in these fields, and there is a consensus that this is possible and important, but that it requires the coupling of education with personal support and guidance on an ongoing basis.

Furthermore, many initiatives have effects which are indirect and difficult to measure. Thus the PAJO project appears to have been successful in transforming the attitudes of employers to young people from immigrant communities, including small firms which had not previously considered employing such people. Certainly the project had succeeded in attracting national media attention and generating positive stories about immigrant young people. The effect of this in cultural change, and social integration may be much more substantial than the handful of jobs directly filled, though these are themselves important for the individuals concerned.

_109|_

A further issue concerns the role of the municipalities. Much is being staked on their role in developing local strategies, and clearly some are developing imaginative approaches. However, doubts were expressed about whether all municipalities, even with grouping of small ones, will be able to tackle the issues.

A distinctive feature of the approaches examined is their focus on individualised solutions, tailoring support to particular needs of individuals and of employers, their use of mutual support within groups (as with PAJO or the Anna Polak School), and their continuation of individual support after the initial placement in work.

Much of the success of the Nieuw Werk initiative, and of the Anna Polak School relates to their strategy of close linkage with employers and the labour market, and tailoring of training to specific needs, rather than to generic programmes. The REGI-OMet project liaises closely with the Regional Foundation of Companies in the Metal Industries, identifying needs, and places where productivity is being blocked by lack of skilled labour, and then negotiating individuals into specific roles, as permanent workers, as "Melkert workers" in subsidised posts, or on training placements. The Anna Polak School staff are in constant contact with employers, looking for new niches in the labour market for their trainees, and producing graduates who have both broad generic employability skills and skills specifically tailored to emerging demands.

The Dutch approach to unemployment, especially as interpreted through Nieuw Werk, appears to the outside observer, a rather severe one. Individuals are approached directly, and offered training leading to employment, probably in a field for which they have no previously expressed interest or experience.

However, some employers clearly feel that recruits trained through the relatively unconventional methods of the WVTCs or the Nieuw Werk programmes are more useful than traditionally trained young people from the vocational system. It is also clear what is needed to do particular jobs, with positive benefits for women and people from immigrant communities.

NORWAY

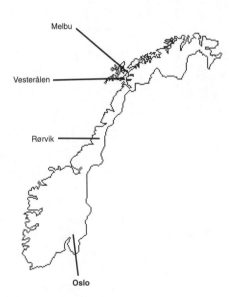

Total population (1996): 4 370 000
– age structure of population 15-64
  (1996): 64.6%;
– age structure of population 65 and over
  (1996): 15.9%.

Land size area: 324 000 sq km.

Per capita GDP (1996 prices): US$36 020.

Annual percentage growth rate (1997): 3.5%.

1997 unemployment rate: 3.2%
– proportion unemployed for 12 months or
  more: 12.8%.

**Expenditure on education per student
(1995):** US$6 360.

**Percentage of population aged 25-64 with
at least upper secondary education:** 81%.

Sources: OECD (1998*h*), *Employment Outlook*;
"OECD in Figures – 1998"; OECD (1998*g*),
Education at a Glance.

" This is about more than learning at work, much more. When I started, I thought: 'Yes , I want
to improve my skills; yes, I want to keep my job.' When I left school, I thought: 'That's it, I've
stopped my learning.'
When I started the work programme, I was a bit nervous at first. Now, I find I keep looking at
the college prospectus – we all do – and keep asking: 'What do I do next?' Yes, we have come
to understand the importance of lifelong learning."

Middle-aged worker at the communications company Telenor Mobile describing how a training
scheme to prevent redundancy led to the creation of a workplace lifelong learning society.

Norway

Context

Norway is a wealthy country rich in natural resources: forestry, fishing, and oil – the country's biggest export industry. Since 1993, the economy has expanded at twice the rate of OECD countries generally. Its commitment to education is strong: in 1997 Norway spent 6.8 per cent of its Gross Domestic Product on public education – the highest of all OECD countries.

High unit costs for education are inevitable in a land so sparsely peopled. The population of 4.3 million is widely spread in cities, small towns and rural communities. Thousands of islands are scattered along the coast, which is deeply indented by fjords; mountains and plateaux cover the interior. The country measures 2 540 km north to south, almost the distance from the North Sea to the Mediterranean. Norway covers an area of 387 000 sq. kilometres, an average of just 13 people per square kilometre.

Industries with large numbers of low-skill jobs such as fish processing are scattered along the complicated coastline. Construction is a very big area of employment in a land where hundreds of bridges link the islands; computing and telecommunications are fast-growing industries. The production of distance-learning materials is also a burgeoning and potentially huge business. Automation is gradually eliminating the low-skill jobs, and there is big growth in the service sector, where government statistics show that 67 per cent of the workforce is employed. Another 20 per cent is found in industry and the rest in fishing farming and forestry. With very low unemployment of 2.8 per cent, the labour market is very tight; shortages are filled in some areas, particularly construction, by immigrant workers, recruited from Denmark, Finland and Sweden.

Norway's booming economy masks the problems it faces in attempting to combat exclusion. The country missed out largely on the industrial revolution that swept Europe in the 17th and 18th centuries and moved swiftly from an agrarian to an advanced nation economically. Export of steel and aluminium, the oil boom and other abundant natural resources have sustained wealth without the need to address too rigorously the question of skills training. Indeed, some of the prosperous industries such as fish processing and forestry are characterised by low skills.

But the Norwegians have proved a remarkably adaptive nation: witness, for example, their rapid growth in the computer software export markets. The government responded to the new skills challenges of the 1980s and 1990s by devolving responsibility, funds and power to the counties and municipalities. In this, the government was not attempting to shift the burden elsewhere; it was taking the historical perspective of a diverse sparsely populated nation that has long been a conglomeration of small communities.

Over the past 20 years, like much of northern Europe, Norway has become considerably more multicultural with the arrival of immigrants, particularly from Pakistan and Turkey. As Norway is a relatively homogeneous society, language has become a barrier to both social and economic inclusion for many immigrants. Measures have been taken to help people adjust. There are also 30 000 Sami, a well-established ethnic minority with its own language and culture with the right to decide between Norwegian or its own tongue as first or second language in school.

Affluence and an increase in mobility of the population over the past two decades have wrought considerable social change, not least a dramatic breakdown in the traditional family structure. As in most European countries, divorce rates have risen sharply in Norway: of all the marriages since 1994, 46 per cent are likely to end in separation, leaving many single-parent families dependent on the state (case study No. 1). There is also a growing migration of the young in search of work, from rural areas to the larger towns and cities, compounding the problems of rural decline. As for most of Europe, Norway has an ageing population profile, increasing the strain on health and social services.

Economic forecasts predict a slowing of economic growth in 1999, as the Norwegian government calculates that employment will increase by just 0.5 per cent a year until 2002. The state cannot meet all the costs of measures to combat exclusion; the government's social partners, the employers and workers organisations including the Confederation of Business and Industry and the Trades Union Congress, will have to invest more resources in lifelong learning.

Norway has a long-standing tradition of adult education for its own sake, with strong emphasis on equality of access. To deny many people the chance to learn would itself be a form of social exclusion. But adult education is increasingly taking a more vocational imperative to give people new competencies and skills for work. Questions are being asked such as "Can a tradition of liberal education be adapted for such a purpose?"; "Are the distance learning tools which are used to retrain people at work flexible enough to assist the unemployed and other excluded groups who lack access to technology?"; "Should the focus be on economic or social exclusion – or both?"

The Norwegian Institute of Adult Education is addressing these and other fundamental questions, many of which have yet to be researched in the context of Norway. Some preliminary answers to questions are found in studies from other Nordic countries. They find that social and economic inclusion are crucial not just to independence but to good health, self-esteem and political involvement.

Problems of exclusion in Norway

Norway faces the two classic challenges of advanced industrial nations: returning the unemployed and socially vulnerable groups to productive work, and preventing whole sectors of the workforce, skilled and unskilled, from slipping into redundancy. Given the dynamics of the labour market and rapidly increasing demands for new skills, both groups are in danger of becoming economically and socially excluded.

Around 70 000 people are registered as unemployed in Norway. Significant numbers are also vulnerable to exclusion, such as one-parent families dependent on social insurance. Financial support for these groups is generous; single parents receive up to NKr 12 500 (US$1 750) a month for child benefits, clothing, food and housing.

The main barriers to economic inclusion are seen by the government, social partners and most providers of adult education as being poor education, lack of skills and competencies and outdated knowledge. Arguments for investment to combat exclusion are, therefore, very strongly in favour of increased adult learning opportunities. Four out of ten people in the workforce never completed upper secondary education; most lack suitable training in the skills needed today. The increasing demand for skills and qualifications means that those not in a position to take part in education and training are disadvantaged as rapid changes in technology eliminate low-skill jobs.

All working-age people are entitled to study up to and through upper secondary level under new government reforms. The state will meet tuition costs for primary and upper secondary, but not the living expenses. Some employers say they will meet these costs; study loans will also be available. Annual negotiations between employers and unions also involve a trade-off between pay and employers committing more money for in-service training to prevent redundancy.

Vulnerable groups – single parents, immigrants, refugees, low-skill workers, the disabled, drug abusers, long-term unemployed (out of work longer than six months) and some made redundant in late middle life – are finding increasing difficulties taking part in both social and working life. Trends among these groups are a cause for concern, say government officials. The burden to the taxpayer of these groups is often bigger than that of the unemployed.

While unemployment has fallen sharply since 1993, long-term (6 months) and youth unemployment persist, at 26.6 per cent and 12.4 per cent respectively (of the total registered unemployed). Government figures put unemployment at 3.2 per cent for 1997. But among immigrants, percentage unemployment rates by county of origin are often considerably higher: Those from Nordic countries and Western Europe (at 4.5 per cent) and North America (5.0 per cent) are nearest the national average. But numbers are substantially higher for other groups: South and Latin America (15.9 per cent), Asia (16.8 per cent), Eastern Europe (17.1 per cent) and Africa (21.5 per cent). Long-term unemployment also occurs more frequently among immigrants than it does among the population in total.

There is still a need to take a wider view of social exclusion than that based on needs of the job market. Studies underway by the Norwegian Institute of Adult Learning suggest that there is an urgent need to address the influence of prior school experiences, to find ways to help adults "unlearn" negative emotional reactions. The result, according to the institution, is not just a negative attitude to work but a fear of participation socially and subsequent exclusion from cultural knowledge, democracy and broader social interaction.

Staff at the institute have been studying a range of research, including work in Sweden dating back to the 1970s, where efforts to use adult education to rehabilitate ex-offenders failed because of the lack of wider social and moral under-pinning of efforts by the authorities. Many studies since the early 1980s could be used in devising programmes to tackle social exclusion but research is still in its infancy.

Adult learning and social exclusion

Development of adult learning is closely linked to the growth of voluntary, cultural and charitable organisations which supported co-operative action. Information activities, lectures, courses and more formal training were the principal tools in the fight for social equality and the political involvement of different sections of society throughout the 20th century. Considerations of personal development, individual progress and democratic participation continue to find expression in lifelong learning. The authorities stress the right to basic education and training for work and further learning. Coupled with this is a tradition of decentralised decision-making and commitment to reducing geographical and social inequalities. Hence the willingness of people to accept with few questions the relatively high government costs of educating a small population.

There is a long tradition of non-governmental organisations (NGOs) taking part in adult education. The biggest are the Folk University and the Workers' Educational Association of Norway (AOF). Founded in 1931, mainly to give extra-mural tuition (*folkeplysning*) to people with little or no formal education, the AOF was licensed by the government in 1993 to issue diplomas in vocational training. It is behind some of the key projects in Norway to find ways of combating exclusion (see case studies No. 1 and 2).

In 1997, more than NKr 2.3 billion was spent by government on adult education and the labour training market. The NGOs attract only a small amount of the cash – most of which goes to the public institutions – and depend on the participant or employer paying. The eagerness of people to continue learning and their willingness to pay is reflected in the recruitment figures. The study associations including the AOF run courses for 750 000 people a year – a quarter of the adult population. Folk Schools and distance-education institutions also became important providers of adult education in post-war Norway. The very broad public commitment was important in raising motivation and encouraging the recruitment of adults for further education. Efforts throughout the second half of the century to raise the status of adult education were very successful. In the 1950s, apprentice reforms ensured improved vocational and workplace study for school leavers. Moves to encourage greater uptake and a broader range of adult learning options came in 1976 with the Adult Education Act, regulating all the areas of public-funded adult education. A wider range of institutions was allowed to offer courses and adults were encouraged to register as ordinary pupils or students at educational institutions. The 1976 act came after considerable public debate over disturbing research evidence of links between low educational achievement and high unemployment.

Weaknesses in the entire education system were gradually exposed through the 1970s and 1980s; it was coming under strain with rapid increase in numbers of students staying on at schools and colleges which were urgently in need of curriculum reform. While liberal studies in adult education were thriving, vocational training and the preparation of school leavers for work were not. New jobs using information technology were growing rapidly as the country emerged from recession in 1993. Norway was facing a skills shortage, and increasing numbers of people were becoming vulnerable to social and economic exclusion.

Main policy approaches

The government has set its national policy sights on returning people to work while retaining a tight grip on fiscal policies. It is also encouraging schemes down to municipal government level (where the welfare safety net operates), to mount projects aimed at releasing a wide range of groups, such as one-parent families, from state dependency.

By the early 1990s, school reform was identified by the Ministry of Education as the most pressing area for change. Numbers staying on for upper secondary level had almost doubled between 1978 and 1992, from 135 000 to 255 000. But the curriculum had not changed to keep in step with the wider ability range. And so Reform

1994 was instituted – a package of measures designed to raise the status of vocational training, defer the age at which students specialise, cut drop-out rates and upgrade studies to meet future challenges. The government called for apprenticeships to be made more flexible to help trainees become adaptable to jobs in the future and the message of lifelong learning was impressed on young people. The focus was altogether more entrepreneurial.

There were more than 100 foundation courses available. Some were extremely narrow, closing rather than opening career doors. The range was cut back to 13 broader programmes, leaving pupils with wider options for trade studies or for further and higher education. Three years free education or vocational training were granted to all 16 to 19-year-olds who wanted it. The reforms were built round a common core curriculum of Norwegian, English, maths, natural science, history and social science. Special measures were introduced to help disadvantaged students and a statutory follow-up service would track drop-outs.

Something had to be done too for the 40 per cent of adults who had not completed the equivalent of the Upper Secondary education, for it was here that the spiral of decline into exclusion was most likely. A 20-year review of participation in adult education, by the Norwegian Institute of Adult Education, revealed a 50 per cent increase since 1976 in numbers of adults involved full-time or part-time in education or training. Numbers of people on work-related courses had risen three-fold But the least educated at school were the first to quit adult education courses, leaving them even more vulnerable to exclusion.

Government policies for lifelong learning carried with them exhortations to employers to assume greater responsibility for more flexible skills training in-company. Annual pay bargaining between the social partners – the unions and employer associations – should yield a trade off between pay rises and cash set aside for such training. Such proposals were being considered during the OECD visit in mid 1998. A series of ambitious government measures had also been introduced to help weak groups such as the disabled and long-term unemployed back to work. Progress was being made: of the one-in four adults in education each year, a quarter are reckoned to be on in-service training.

County authorities which have responsibility for upper secondary education were required – for every four students aged 16 to 19 in the schools and colleges – to keep an additional place open in order to give adults an opportunity to return to the classroom. The authorities were also expected to exploit more fully the decentralisation that had been introduced in 1986. Grants which used to be earmarked for primary and secondary education were replaced by a lump sum to cover the range of services: education, cultural and social and transport and communications. Municipal and county councils are asked to co-ordinate these services and create projects in order to improve the support given to disadvantaged groups. Schools and colleges have been freed to offer courses commercially, adding resources to public funds and stimulating co-operation between education and business, as in a staff skills training project involving the phone company Telenor Mobile and Trondheim University (see case study No. 3).

Proposed entitlements were spelled out in the autumn of 1997 in a government consultation paper: New Competence – the basis for a total policy for continuing education and training for adults. It proposed new non-formal routes to higher education for those without qualifications, based on competence and proven ability.

A government White Paper was passed in May 1998, with plans to offer training to all adults who had not reached upper secondary education standard, with a statutory right to study leave. The state meets the costs of lower-level education for adults who need to catch up. A national student loan scheme is proposed, with a review of taxation rules to encourage lifelong learning.

Three proposals to prevent social and economic exclusion among adults are: the introduction of new types of non-formal assessment leading to a qualification (accreditation of prior learning); a right to basic education for all who need it; and a training contract between employers and unions, with funds set aside through agreements.

It is also adopting a carrot-and-stick approach. A tougher line is being taken on benefits payments to encourage vulnerable groups to take advantage of education and training initiatives. It is for the councils, the social partners and the education organisations to decide how best to apply the regulations to meet local needs. The government has revived and refined the Youth Guarantee of education or employment.

Case studies

Case study 1

Project: single parents returning to the labour force.

Starting date: 1995.

Organisation in charge: partnership of local government and AOF.

Location: Vesteralen.

A small group of single mothers was determined to have adult learning courses designed to suit its needs after the government had introduced welfare-to-work legislation linking social benefits to attendance at work or college. The group's success led to national acclaim for a scheme that has since been copied throughout Norway.

Overview

The costs of childcare benefits, healthcare and welfare for single-parent families have escalated with the decline of the traditional family structure in Norway.

With 46 per cent of marriages since 1994 predicted to break up, it is overtaking Britain in having the highest divorce rate of Europe. Half the 50 000 single parents depend on state and municipal services. The financial burden on just one municipality, Sortland, in the sparsely populated northern region of Vesteralen, is NKr 13 million a year. A dependent parent with two children receives NKr 150 000 (US$21 000) social insurance a year. Regardless of the costs, the authorities were increasingly concerned over the cycle of dependency that parents – overwhelmingly mothers – and their children were trapped in. Parents without work or a place at college were often socially very isolated. Welfare-to-work measures were regarded as necessary to combat social exclusion.

In 1995, a co-operative was formed between the local authorities (social welfare, employment and insurance benefits) and the Workers' Educational Association for Norway (AOF) to promote initiatives to make parents self-sufficient and break the cycle of deprivation. A project was launched to prepare and motivate single parents for the employment market, following a passive period claiming insurance. Many young mothers had lost self-confidence and needed constant motivation and support to stay in education or training. The project uses co-ordinated services to help families build new lives. By mid-1998, around 580 women from five municipalities had participated in the project, in which education and support service are tailored to individual needs. One such project is *Regineklassen*, an education initiative in Sortland to give women the necessary formal competencies for college or university study or a job.

Projects

One mother, Sissel Frydstad refused to accept the bureaucratic regulations when told that her group of three single mothers was too small to form an adult education class in Sortland. Future welfare benefits rested on their taking up education or work. They were angry that they seemed to be offered little choice. Rather than give in, they formed a mutual-support group and phoned everyone they knew in the same predicament. Within 12 hours they had rallied 22 ready to sign up for a customised course leading to upper secondary school certificate.

Sissel's story became famous through national TV coverage. The AOF responded swiftly, giving over an entire floor of its Sortland offices for classrooms, private study areas, social rooms for staff and students. It was equipped and decorated by the mothers and staff with a small local authority budget, AOF support and voluntary help. Two trained teachers were allocated, giving generous student-teacher contact time. The mutual support network became a fixture, with the students encouraging each other constantly to stay the course in difficult times. A challenging curriculum covered six subjects to advanced level – maths, natural science, social studies, history, Norwegian and English – with individualised support services to help prevent drop-outs.

Two similar projects were started in the south of Vesteralen following a general assessment of the first intake in Sortland. A second year had recruited 16 single parents in Sortland and the AOF was in negotiations with the Ministry of Health and Social Affairs for a 2 million NKr grant to expand and improve the programme.

Outcomes

In Sortland, all but one of the first intake passed their exams and went on to further study or training for jobs ranging from hairdressing and pre-school teaching to social work, and teaching older children. Sissel passed a further certificate in philosophy and secured a university place to study medicine.

Earlier efforts to encourage parents back to learn failed because the classic school setting was inappropriate or intimidating. Schools have come to recognise this; two in neighbouring counties have reformed their entire curriculum management in the light of Sortland's experience.

The municipal authorities responsible have a 75 per cent success rate in returning parents to work through study, as against the national average of 65 per cent. The level of success impressed the government since the co-operative which enabled it to happen was a direct community response to policies to combat exclusion. Full welfare, social support and child welfare benefits were formerly available to single parents until the child was ten. From this year, however, when a child is three, the parent's benefits depend on their taking work or education.

Sortland's project illustrates how fears and prejudices associated with early failures are quickly overcome when flexible teaching and learning, and an "adult" environment are provided. None of the women interviewed found the return to study easy. Sissel was typical; with four children, she had to manage the AOF centre studies in the morning and cram private study in late at night, when the children were in bed. All the women referred, however, to the "fun" of learning. Nevertheless, there are severe limitations, which the AOF staff and co-operating authorities insist the government must address in the longer term. The first year was a uniquely driven group; the second had more of a struggle. The teachers believe the upper secondary school level – which the government demands if the course is to qualify for cash – is too high for at least five of the group. For a minority, the demands are too challenging and preparatory studies are needed; for many, the time scale is too short. From 1998 teachers have phased the work over two years. But the biggest drawback with rapid expansion in recruitment is the class sizes. Staff insist that more teachers are needed to ensure much smaller groups and more individual attention.

121

The self-help perspective is seen as very important. Already the methods developed through the Sortland project are being applied to other groups. Through a series of education programmes former drug abusers are using the supportive techniques to help others off drugs. The Sortland AOF staff said a longer-term evaluation was needed to assess whether the parents' successes could can continue through university.

The message from local officials to the government is that in the strongly decentralised political system of Norway, integration of health, employment and social welfare is needed. The current approach leaves resources too fragmented, in a situation where individuals in danger of exclusion exhibit a multitude of different problems.

Case study 2

Project: preventing redundancy through ill-health in the fish processing industry.
Organisation in charge: AOF.
Location: Melbu.

Reforms aimed at cutting extraordinarily high levels of exclusion resulting from industrial injury and ill-health redundancy in fish processing plants have been agreed upon by management and unions. The model education, training and job rotation programme is being studied by other physically-demanding industries in the Nordic countries.

Overview

Rapid expansion of the fishing industry brought hundreds of jobs in processing plants to the islands of the north-west coastal region of Vesteralen in the 1950s. High-pay, low-skill jobs were plentiful in one of Norway's fastest expanding export industries.

But the rewards came at a terrible cost to health. A large proportion of the Norwegian fish processing industry is still staffed by workers characterised as unskilled. The highest paid piece-rate jobs such as filleting the fish are repetitive, boring, and physically destructive. Within three weeks of starting work, the average employee often complains of crippling musculo-skeletal pains in the hands and back. Absenteeism is rife; physiotherapy costly. In some plants, the majority of workers who do not escape the drudgery are on disability pensions ten to 15 years before official retirement age. There is a widespread impression of the fishing industry being "bad" work. This reinforces a lack of self-confidence and low self-esteem in a workforce characterised for the most part by low educational achievement.

Now, staff face an equally appalling prospect of redundancy and long-term unemployment, as automation will eliminate jobs which, even though they are low-skill tasks, are among those with the best rates of pay. Efforts by employers to counter disaffection and improve performance have not resulted in significant advances or increased willingness among workers to change their practices.

As part of a project on barriers to unskilled workers taking part in company training, the Workers Educational Association of Norway (AOF) has carried out two case studies in the Norwegian fish industry; one in Vesteralen, the other on the west coast. Two major employers allowed their working practices to be closely scrutinised in an effort to understand the training needs for the 21st century and to halt a spiral of decline in health and employability.

Projects

Under the 1980 Vocational Training Act all employees are encouraged to gain a recognised trade certificate. A large proportion of the fishing industry workforce has still to do so. The AOF study found low self-esteem and some negative experiences at school putting people off later study. Disaffection with work rather than a positive attitude to the job was the prime motivating force for those who chose to do further studies. Trade union sponsored courses were over-subscribed, not because the staff wanted new skills but because they wanted to escape work. Relationships between managers and workers became strained, and employers distrusted the motives of staff and were disinclined to release them for further study.

The study indicated that few people starting jobs were interested in hard physical work, and rapid onset of health problems increased disaffection. Efforts by companies to rotate jobs and cut health risks failed as those who were retrained monopolised "softer" jobs, reducing options for rotation. Those unable to develop their jobs asked why they should do more study.

A questionnaire for the study revealed that many women would rather do "men's" work such as driving. But there are strong stereotypes and expectations in Norway – another barrier to job rotation – though this is changing. Evidence also emerged of strategies among older workers to cling to the easier work.

Middle managers responsible for training, in the larger of the two companies in the AOF study, were aware of the need for training but failed to convince top management who controlled budgets. And so, nothing was done. The smaller, family firm, had never invested in training; the owners feared that it would create exorbitant wage demands. Workers who had a trade certificate were never able to use it to advance within the firm. Further recruitment problems followed, with the vicious circle of health problems worsening.

Problems were not all with management. Many workers did not want to change jobs if it meant leaving friends made at work. Many, making good money on jobs such as filleting did not want to change to the fixed rates of pay on washing and packaging. And so, when one factory tried to start a retraining programme for the trade certificate with skilled workers, no one came forward. In the Vesteralen plant of 240 workers, just two volunteered to retrain. In the sister plant, 17 came forward.

The management was stunned by the findings of the AOF study. But at the Vesteralen Melbu plant owners have now set about a radically new training regime in partnership with the unions and AOF to help employees gain a certificate for what they have learned in the workplace. New workers are given an initial 12 weeks training for at least two hours a week. Those doing repetitive tasks will have better initial training and physiotherapy. The new machinery coming in will require people with a more technical background. Management is monitoring more closely which manual jobs are likely to go and when. Staff will be trained for these changes.

Outcomes

The fish processing industry has produced a model for retraining which is being studied by similar physically-demanding industries throughout Norway. The owners, managers and workers admit that there is a pressing need for better training. Without it the very future of the plants could be at risk as buyers, in an increasingly health-conscious country, are ready to put pressure on producers. In the short term, factories which fail to guarantee that at least 40 per cent of staff have the trade certificates of skilled workers will lose trade, because of minimum demands on standards planned by the buyers.

To help overcome the reluctance of staff to retrain, the companies are seeking ways to offer better pay for jobs other than the piece-rate tasks. This should also encourage job rotation and alleviate health problems. It is accepted by employers and unions alike that this will take time. But the ultimate goal now is to give staff multiple skills for a range of tasks from the start of training. The companies will spell out in their strategies for the coming years that staff who retrain will be given opportunities to use their new skills.

Very similar repetitive work practices, which cause ill-health, tedium and under-achievement, are found in the forestry-related trades and crafts such as window frame production. In the neighbouring Danish textiles industry, employers have kept up levels of employment and improved health by retraining people to use computerised technology which was replacing the old handicraft skills such as sewing. In fact, those with the old craft skills, knowledge of and "feel" for textiles control the computerised processes more effectively and efficiently than those without these competencies.

Case study 3

Project: workers with out-dated competencies – telecommunications.

Starting date: 1996.

Organisation in charge: partnership of Telenor Mobile, Trondheim University and colleges.

Location: Rørvik.

An initiative to update the competences of highly-skilled but vulnerable workers in the fast-changing telecommunications industry has also created a wide range of new jobs for the unemployed. Every employee on the programme has since asked to sign-up for further studies at the local college or through distance learning at Trondheim University and the unique public-private partnership has been acclaimed as a model to promote lifelong learning through the workplace.

Overview

Nowhere has the content of work changed more dramatically than in telecommunications. Little remains of the technical competencies that workers in this field learned at school. New service industry jobs proliferate; employees need both advanced technical skills and personal aptitudes to deal with customers on a global scale.

Such industries show no respect for geographical and political boundaries. Countries which fail to capitalise on new information technologies will be the poorer nations of the 21st century, providing the cheap labour "down line" to others which control the new means of post-industrial production.

Telenor Mobile, a department of the Norwegian Telephone Company, started in 1876 as a telegraphic service. For 100 years there was virtually no change in the largely technician employment patterns. Then, in 14 years from the mid-1980s it grew from 40 000 subscribers to 1.2 million. There was a five-fold increase in jobs with a shift from technician to customer services. New job demands ranged from the processing of 6 million bills a year to collection of cash from defaulters and tackling new crimes such as theft through the cloning of mobile phones. Increasingly seen as a major player in the US$70 billion industry, Telenor has customers as far afield as Bangladesh. New speed and flexibility is needed not only in processing information but in the turn-around of products. But even with the volume of work, survival of the company cannot be guaranteed without constant investment in staff skills training to cope with the speed of change.

The company is based in Rørvik, on the coastline in mid-Norway. Rørvik is a small village with few companies and with difficulties in building up new industry. Due to the long distances, companies and employees in the countryside have

125

problems upgrading their knowledge at a college or university. It takes five hours to drive from the village to the nearest university. A distance learning project was therefore established in collaboration with the Norwegian Technical University in Trondheim and the local upper secondary school. The project's importance is not just in relation to upgrading skills but also for individual job survival and possibly that of the company, a key employer in the community. The problem was how to upgrade the skills of existing workers and fill new posts as they emerge. Using the Internet, workers could have a university education without leaving their home, local school or workplace. The two-year project is a forerunner to bigger, government-backed initiatives which could transform the way a large proportion of adults learn. Telenor Mobile gives workers 50 per cent paid time to study up to degree level. At the time of the OECD visit, 25 workers were taking part in the programme.

Projects

Individuals in the project are trained to take greater responsibility for a range of jobs demanding higher standards of education, in a market where at least half the new jobs globally will be at degree level. Telenor Mobile instructors work closely with the university, local upper school and Norwegian Institute of Business. Co-operation with the municipal and county authorities is also essential for effective use of resources in such a sparsely populated area.

Students from the work place can gain 20 credits a year (maximum 25 over two years) towards a higher-level university qualification, without ever leaving Rørvik. They are linked on-line from the workplace and home computers to tutors who give the same range of teaching, technical and pastoral support services that they give students based at the university.

Telenor Mobile staff on the project study economics, computer sciences and business English, having to reacquire all to degree level. A system of accreditation of prior learning is used to exempt them from having to reacquire skills, knowledge and competencies already gained. As skills shortages cannot be met fast enough through new recruitment, and people leave for larger conurbations if dissatisfied with progress at work, the company recognises that more in-service training must be provided.

The project is boosted by a key initiative of the government to fight unemployment. For every five students given day release, Telenor Mobile takes on a substitute worker for ten months under the Job Seeker scheme. It is expected that if substitutes show aptitude and interest, they will be taken on full-time at the end and trained in the higher-level skills as job opportunities grow. Telenor had taken on five such workers at the time of the OECD study visit in 1998.

The project is therefore a specific response to the call for initiatives from central government. Its three main objectives are to:

- help employers restructure organisations and boost local job growth and recruitment;
- prevent information workers from becoming redundant;
- help job seekers find quality work and training.

The Telenor Mobile story gives only part of the picture. The other main players are the upper school and university. The Norwegian Technical University in Trondheim has substantially increased its use of information technology in distance learning for the past decade since an OECD 1988 conference on the subject.

Norway has a long tradition of open learning to reach a sparsely populated population. In 1994, the university launched what became the Norway-net with IT for Open Learning (NITOL). Initially through telephone links and later the Internet and World Wide Web, it collaborates with three further education colleges. In 1998, it recruted 1 700 distance learners a term from four main target groups: university and college students, professionals, individuals and companies (particularly small and medium enterprises) and systems managers in universities, colleges and schools looking to expand their knowledge and skills.

NITOL aims to provide at a modest cost, anywhere in Norway, a "one-stop shop" for all education and competence-training needs. The aim eventually is to open the network to any institution, study centre, school, college, voluntary organisation or social partner such as the Folk University or Workers' Educational Association, to provide any necessary local support needed to back up the distance learning. Logically, there would be no need for any central organisation or headquarters other than for administration. The plan is for a Virtual Learning University to establish permanent links with all customers, including the pathfinder businesses in the distance learning programme such as Telenor Mobile

Outcomes

The Telenor-Trondheim work has proved to be a considerable success on many fronts. Job skills have improved to match the rapidly changing demands, and jobs taken by substitute workers have been converted into permanent posts. An unexpected gain is the high level of commitment to lifelong learning among staff who have studied on the Telenor programme. Everyone who had completed a course said they intended to study further, not just for work but for a whole range of social and educational reasons. One employee likened the offices of Telenor Mobile to a class of the university.

The Upper Secondary School staff said they had noticed a big increase in inquiries for courses from people working in Telenor. Seven Telenor employees from the first intake for the programme said they were looking to further studies, either at the local school or through distance learning at the university. Their study plans ranged from computer sciences to art and foreign languages. One woman in her 40s commented: "When I left school, I really thought that was that as far as my studying went. When I started to do the retraining here, it was a question of keeping my job. Now it is so much more; the social contacts too."

Job satisfaction had increased substantially, not only for full-time staff but also for substitute workers who recognised that they had a better deal than many of their unemployed friends. With the increased opportunities locally, community leaders hope that projects such as the Telenor-Trondheim scheme will discourage people, particularly young people, from seeking work elsewhere.

The ability to study to a very high level locally is another consideration. Regulations require universities to charge the same for courses, whether they be lecture-based or taught at a distance. The intention here is to prevent options being eroded and students being channelled down inappropriate roads just because they are cheaper. Conversely, the universities must not be allowed to escalate costs beyond what small firms can afford. The government is mindful that if more accessible and effective teaching methods aimed at the home and work place are developed through projects such as the Telenor Mobile scheme, they must be universally available and accessible.

At regional level, the county council is financing schemes on the lines of the Telenor project model to help small and medium enterprises collaborate in cost-effective in-service training. Longer term it is generally accepted that initiatives will succeed only if new companies as well as new jobs created meet the range of new consumer options telematics can offer.

Innovations and effectiveness

Norway's projects are models of flexibility and negotiation, which led to some considerable successes. Three notable achievements stand out in analysing the projects:

- – A very flexible approach to the regulations on the part of local and central government helped single parents take their own adult learning initiative. The broad partnership which was formed to support them, helped design an alternative education framework that won national acclaim and was adopted in other parts of the country.

- – Norway has created a highly original model of retraining and education to save hundreds of workers from redundancy and motivate them at work. Industrial health reforms designed within the framework of an adult learning programme were made possible only by the full commitment from all partners in a joint private-public sector initiative.

- The information technology skills course at Telenor Mobile has done more than save workers from redundancy. It has injected new life and jobs into an isolated community and turned a workplace into a lifelong learning centre.

Commentary

The case studies illustrate the extent to which the line between social and economic exclusion in Norway is blurred. The country's leading adult education institution has warned of the dangers in taking too narrow a view of exclusion (focusing on employment). Indeed, the approaches to tackling exclusion are clearly employment led, with a strong emphasis on issues on returning people to work (the single mothers of Vesteralen) or preventing exclusions from the workplace (the fish processing plant in Melbu).

But, while questions of employability are uppermost, there is a clear and rapidly growing perception of the causes of social exclusion being far wider than a mere question of economics. All three case studies revealed a willingness among clients, workers, community groups, NGOs and government at both local and national level to change direction and rethink the rules where it suits the individuals and the communities involved. This probably stems from the fact that while Norway is very much a nation of individuals, often isolated and living predominantly in small communities, the geography and social mix of the country dictates a community response to so many issues.

The case studies also illustrate the importance of partnerships. Without them, there can be no dialogue. The Melbu fishing industry project offers a remarkable insight into how the entrenched social attitudes of individuals have sustained some of the most preposterous working practices. This is not the case of an autocratic employer wanting production on the cheap; it is the attitudes of workers who want to stick with their friends and who put short-term cash interests before their health. It was not enough to identify the problems, as the research did; agreement among all parties on a longer-term strategy was necessary.

Where Norway succeeds is in offering real incentives. It may come with a "carrot and stick" warning of reduced welfare benefits, as in the Vesteralen one-parent family project; it may carry the promise of personal and professional enhancement, as does the Telenor Mobile project in Rørvik. The latter, incidentally, gives an added bonus: everyone who passes the examinations can keep the expensive computers for home use.

The projects also touch the lives of participants; the projects are decentralised, locally driven, and yet have the active support of central government. Self-motivation

129

is tapped and nurtured through mutual support groups. The remarkable support network in Sissel's story in the first case study may be unusual; subsequent groups, however, appear to be following their lead.

There is also a collective will to succeed. In Sortland, NGOs such as the Workers Educational Association of Norway (AOF), county and municipal authorities and the health, education, employment and welfare services all contribute and give constant backing; some even helped equip and redecorate the project "school" in the AOF offices where cash was scarce. The AOF wants more money; the local authorities want even more devolved power to run the multiple support services under one roof. Nevertheless, the constant message to the single parents is: each individual matters. So too with Telenor Mobile: Trondheim University, the local upper secondary school, county authorities and employers to top management level are constantly willing staff to succeed and opening real opportunities for substitute workers, thereby cutting unemployment.

While there are unique geographic, demographic, political and economic circumstances in Norway, many countries could learn something from the three projects, because they are about social and human values as much as fiscal and job considerations. Less affluent, more densely populated countries would have difficulty since the Norway schemes carry a comparatively high level of cash support for families during education and training (though this is being eroded). However, non-financial considerations such as partnership and agreed frameworks for action account for a substantial part of the successes.

As with many successful initiatives, the projects often had unexpected spin-offs, such as the creation of a lifelong learning environment at Telenor Mobile and the extension of new types of adult learning to other communities following the success of the one-parent adult learning programme.

PORTUGAL

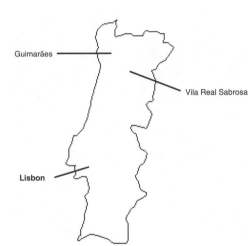

Guimarães

Vila Real Sabrosa

Lisbon

Total population (1996): 9 935 000
– age structure of population 15-64 (1996): 67.7%;
– age structure of population 65 and over (1996): 14.8%.

Land size area: 92 000 sq km.

Per capita GDP (1996 prices): US$10 425.

Annual percentage growth rate (1997): 3.5%.

1997 unemployment rate: 6.8%
– proportion unemployed for 12 months or more: 55.6%.

Expenditure on education per student: No OECD data.

Percentage of population aged 25-64 with at least upper secondary education: 20%.

Sources: OECD (1998*h*), *Employment Outlook*; "OECD in Figures – 1998"; OECD (1998*g*), *Education at a Glance*.

" When I was seven, my schoolteacher said: 'I want you to come and work for me in my house, you don't need to go to school, I will teach you to read there.' But she never did teach me. Since the child-minding project started classes, I have begun to learn at last, and now I can write my name. Does my husband approve? No he doesn't, but I have been denied the right to learn for 60 years; I am not going to let him stop me now."

Statement from a woman in a childminder's reading group in São Tomasao, part of a community development project using literacy to combat social exclusion.

131

Portugal

Context

Portugal is one of the poorest countries in Western Europe. It has the lowest per capita GDP, and is one of the three bottom countries on all the living standards indicators. It shares many characteristics with its wealthier neighbour, Spain, including late urbanisation and rule by dictatorship until the 1970s, but Spain has outpaced it on most indicators in recent years.

Following a bloodless revolution in 1974, Portugal is still emerging from a history of highly centralised government, with poor health and education. Considerable progress has been made but it still has a long way to go in tackling social division and marginalisation. It is a country with a tradition for early school leaving – often as young as ten or 12 years.

Three types of migration also contribute to the divisions in society. A huge influx of people often with low educational levels began in the 1970s with the arrival of 700 000 immigrants from former African colonies. Internal migration from rural to urban life by poorly educated people began in the 1960s and continues, as does a drift outwards of more than 1 million people to work in other European countries. Emigration contributes to the rapid ageing of rural communities. Immigration and the exodus from rural communities have created large urban populations, particularly in Oporto and Lisboa, the capital, with poor educational attainment and low expectations among the second generation. Urban migrants settled either in poor quality social housing or shanty towns. When some shanty towns were cleared recently in a major programme of urban renewal, people were moved close to areas of existing social housing, sometimes physically isolated, and subjected to social stigma.

There are signs of progress with continued decentralisation of government. Big improvements in health have over the past 20 years brought a sharp drop in infant mortality and increased life expectancy (OECD, 1998f). Officially, unemployment is 6.8 per cent and falling (though there is a thriving black market economy) and the national economy was stable enough for Portugal to join the first round of the European Monetary Union. This followed the government's commitment in 1989 to the most radical privatisation programme anywhere in Europe, as 40 state-owned enterprises were sold-off in just seven years, amounting to 14 per cent of GDP.

But this progress has not lifted the barriers to inclusion for sizeable sections of the population, notably in the largest metropolitan area and in rural communities. Almost half the 106 000 agriculture jobs have disappeared since 1986 and while manufacturing has remained buoyant, employing around one third of the workforce, demands for new skills have grown. There has been a corresponding rise in service jobs, including tourism, but many are seasonal and pay lower wages. A big uncertainty in the economy is the size of the "informal" economies. Community-based research into unofficial childcare services in Guimaraes in the north suggests such fringe employment may be more common than believed by officials (case study No. 3). Although a small country of 9.9 million people, Portugal shows strong regional differences in culture and economy, both between rural and urban areas and between the coast and the inland. Some problems, however, are universal, such as low wages and incomes. There is general concern over drug abuse.

Portugal is a society undergoing very rapid change. Some parts are attempting to move in a matter of years through processes of economic and social development which have taken decades in other parts of Europe. This is particularly true in isolated rural communities dependent on subsistence agriculture, and urban migrant communities dependent on marginal employment and the black market economy. The models of education available to tackle this are a sometimes uneasy combination of the old and the very new. Often, radical community development strategies sit alongside an extremely traditional curriculum.

Problems of exclusion in Portugal

Many people do not perceive themselves as "excluded", since they have low expectations of participation and little contact with the world of the "included". This appears to be true of people in both rural and urban communities.

The most serious issue for Portuguese education is that identified by OECD indicators – the low level of school completion in both urban and rural areas. This reflects low expectations, lack of positive role models, low parental education levels, withdrawal of girls from school to care for younger siblings, and in some regions a resistance to "going back to school" by men (and a related reluctance to allow their wives to do so, although some women attend despite this). All these issues affect particularly those who have migrated from the former colonies and from rural areas to cities. The problem is aggravated further by the inflexibility of the housing market which traps people in cheap, poor quality social housing, inherited by second and third generations, maintaining whole communities on a permanent margin. In rural areas, the problem remains general population decline as a result of a lack of policies to revitalise and modernise marginal and subsistence agriculture, coupled with a low education and skills base.

Only one in five Portuguese adults aged 25-64 has completed secondary education, while two thirds have not progressed to second level education at 12; the need for "recurrent education" to bring these adults (and young people) up to a school leaving level dominates much discussion about adult education. Official estimates from one of the country's five administrative regions suggest that one in three adults is socially excluded.

Poor literacy skills, reflected in the low education success rates and stay-on rates, are a major problem in most areas, as demonstrated by a national adult literacy survey in 1995. Considerable efforts have been made to improve literacy levels. By the early 1990s, government estimates suggest that less than 10 per cent of the working population suffer from the severest forms of illiteracy, with problems worse for women than men. However, that is not the whole picture: many adults who left school able to read have long since lost any functional literacy. This excludes access to latest information designed to improve efficiency (and profitability) in agriculture and industry. It also contributes to the cycle of decline as families with poor levels of literacy send young children into primary school ill-prepared for their basic education (case study No. 3).

The Ministry of Education says the main problems identified with social exclusion are:

- early withdrawal from school;
- a high drop out from recurrent (adult) education;
- a history of lower participation among women;
- the ageing population profile in rural areas;
- drug abuse among 25 to 45-year-old men;
- male pride making men reluctant to return to learn.

Adult learning and social exclusion

In Portugal, the term "adult education" is often taken to mean "recurrent education". The meaning in this case is different to that used in most OECD countries; in Portugal it is essentially the teaching of the formal school curriculum to adults who had left school early. Levels of achievement are very low compared with most of Western Europe.

Portugal has lagged considerably behind the rest of Western Europe in education for most of the 20th century. Compulsory schooling for girls from age six was not introduced until 1964, when all children became entitled to six years primary education. Until then, boys had only four years in school. Compulsory schooling for all was further extended to nine years in the mid-1980s, more than a decade after the bloodless revolution of 1974.

After the revolution, the government implemented a policy of lifelong learning and a legal commitment to expanding adult education. More that 2 000 associations were on hand to assist and a Directorate for Adult Education was created within the Ministry of Education. A national ten-year plan for adult literacy and basic education was launched with ambitious targets: 184 000 enrolments a year by 1984 at a cost of almost Esc 400 million. School teachers were offered incentives – guaranteed salaries and a possibility to go back to school – if they switched to adult education. The Directorate set about creating local libraries for new curriculum materials targeted first at the most backward regions. It was hoped that every adult, regardless of economic status, would benefit from a major decentralised programme of community and cultural development.

In practice, only a fraction of the adult population was reached by the end of the 1980s. Resources in a still impoverished nation were scarce; an even more ambitious national plan for the schools was inevitably taking priority. Total school enrolments had doubled to almost 2 million in the 20 years to 1980, with most of the new intake being girls. Overcrowded schools were working shift systems from dawn to dark; scarce resources were being directed to expand schemes such as the already successful telescola, distance education to children who were too few and isolated to warrant more than one or two teachers.

Education for adults is highly segmented. The Ministry for Education is responsible for recurrent education – essentially the delivery of a formal school curriculum to adults who have not completed it before. School-teachers run such classes, and a recent review of this approach reported very high drop-out rates. The Ministry of Employment and Social Solidarity is responsible for courses to improve the qualifications of the long-term and low-skilled adults, to update the professions and also for vocational training schools for young people. Some individual ministries run their own limited training. The universities are responsible for initial and continuing development for professions such as teaching. While they have no formal role in adult education, the universities have an impact through training field workers, providing technical help and researching community needs. For example, the new University at Vila Real established by academic staff returning from the colonies, was a major force in the economic and social regeneration of the city and its surrounds. Its influence is evident in the work at Sabrosa (see case study No. 2). There is no formal training or qualification for those who work in education with adults, although there are short courses offered through the Universities.

Recent community developments to combat exclusion at regional and municipal level of government have succeeded in encouraging more pupils to stay on in school, though there is still a problem of low expectations among some parents who themselves dropped out early. The level of success is reflected in all the case studies at the end of this chapter.

The five regional offices of government act as administrative arms of central ministries, with no delegated powers. However, they co-ordinate an extensive network of education and community development activities geared to local needs which follow many of the initiatives in the 1980s. The regional office in Lisbon, visited during the OECD study, has created teams of staff, usually teachers, to work at sub-regional level on strategies that include recurrent education, pre-vocational programmes, and social and cultural programmes.

Emphasis on community development comes over strongly from the adult education directorates of regional government. They call for a balance between the traditional recurrent education to enter the labour market and for more tailored education "for social participation". The two issues are seen as intertwined. Initiatives across government departments are also called for, with dialogue especially between the Ministry of Labour and Ministry of Education. There is a need for diplomas for young people and adults: formal recognition of achievement, not tied exclusively to traditional educational goals.

Main policy approaches

Current strategies for combating exclusion include measures to pay greater attention to adults who failed to complete nine years schooling. They provide a curriculum that balances vocational training and work experience, leading to a lower-secondary school certificate and vocational diploma. Schools have been given increased autonomy and are encouraged to work more closely with firms. There is also, amongst other active partnership organisations, a Round Table of Industrialists for Education that encourages exchanges between school teachers and company managers. The aims are to foster a more relevant curriculum and to encourage training in the workplace. Under the Minimum Income guarantee, low-paid individuals can join a programme which provides a minimum wage, provided they pursue agreed activities such as basic and pre-school education and family learning. There is increased cross-departmental working in government to educate for social life as well as employment.

137|

A prominent feature of policy in Portugal is the integration of educational, social and work-related initiatives, using a multi-agency approach, combining staff from several Ministries – including Education and Social Solidarity – and the wider employer and community organisations. Funding includes significant sums from the EU for initiatives which promote community self-help and the traditional craft skills – particularly among the young people – which have been shown to raise expectations among children from poorer families and to promote greater self-esteem and self-confidence.

An agency for the general and vocational education of adults has been proposed under a national strategy proposed by the government. This is the major new initiative to create a new semi-autonomous national agency to manage adult continuous learning, including providers in the private sector, and crossing the traditional boundaries between education and labour Ministries. This proposal is currently undergoing widespread consultation.

In 1997, a government-commissioned study of adult education led to a National Task Force and the subsequent national strategy paper that was widely consulted at the time of the OECD visit. The aim is a radical overhaul of the system: to expand the range and coherence of programmes; to increase individual autonomy; to give the private and voluntary sectors a bigger role and to bring together educational services for adults which are currently under different Ministries. The model is similar to that in other parts of Europe, especially the United Kingdom.

The principal proposals are to:
- guarantee adults an education and training equivalent to both a school leaving age level qualification and a certificate of vocational proficiency, tailored to their individual needs;
- create a national network of local learning centres to help overcome personal resistance or isolation and improve access to printed and audio-visual materials;
- give advice, guidance and credit for prior learning gained in areas other than formal school work;
- establish an open learning institution for adults, offering personal tuition and nationally generated materials;
- devise training programmes for adult educators;
- commission research into the most effective adult education methods;
- launch a promotional campaign;
- merge the resources and work of different ministries under the semi-autonomous national Adult Education and Training Agency;

- exploit more effectively the many under-used educational buildings, making local authorities responsible for housing local centres.

Results of the national consultations show that the proposal to merge the work of the two ministries is welcomed. But there were concerns over the need to preserve current good practice and the positions of relevant staff – although all recurrent-education staff are recruited from practising school teachers, and are guaranteed the right to return to work in schools – and about the involvement of the private sector. Areas of particular uncertainty were the status of the national agency – what its legal form should be, how closely it should relate to government – and the nature of the regional dimension.

The government is very conscious of the scale and complexity of the problems. Many proposals in the national strategy are at the leading edge of thinking about the role of adult education in society. Equally, the government is acutely aware of Portugal's position in the OECD education indicators. Indeed, some field workers fear that important community development work may be squeezed out by the need to improve formal education qualification levels to satisfy an external audience. A further evidence of change is the number of new, or relatively new, projects, many of them funded through EU programmes. The speed of these changes makes it particularly difficult to assess the effectiveness of adult education as an instrument of intervention in social exclusion.

The present structure for adult education in Portugal has been in place for more than 20 years and there is much debate about whether it is fundamentally sound but under-resourced, or in need of radical overhaul. The current review encourages an open debate about this, and the proposals include a suggestion that private sector agencies (mostly those of a non-profit-making nature) might also bid to carry out local plans.

While a lack of resources is accepted by government as a key reason why ambitious goals have been missed, there are other equally fundamental factors: a high drop-out rate from a "school" system taught substantially by school teachers and a lack of formal qualifications and training for workers in this field. More research on the education of adults is needed. Despite vigorous networking by some people, there could be wider opportunities to share expertise and knowledge of successful innovation. Some communities have created mini-libraries where printed materials are available, but other small rural community efforts to build literacy are hampered by the absence of adequate material to read.

More attention must be given to open and distance learning – on the lines of the successful telescola for adults and young people within isolated communities seeking more than basic education and training. Concentration of vocational training in larger centres excludes those who must travel excessive distances to develop their skills.

139

There is a general lack of employer involvement in adult learning, but this is changing as private sector influences grow. There are also political changes that make their involvement more imperative. In 1996, a social pact was agreed upon among employers, unions and government. In exchange for moderate wage demands, the government has pledged to increase investment in reforms on a wide range of fronts including education, employment and training.

There is also growing pressure on Portugal from the EU to close the qualifications gap with the rest of Europe. One proposal is a further raising of the school-leaving age and increased work-related training for school drop-outs. If employers don't get involved, they will have to take the staff they are "given". Another pressure from Europe is for the Portuguese government to insist on higher standards of training through improved quality controls.

If the national strategy is implemented in full, then schools and school teachers will take more of a back seat as new breeds of adult enablers, advisers and guidance counsellors would operate through the Adult Education Agency and network of local centres, designing materials and channelling resources to meet very specific community needs. Already, the education of school children is changing as industrialists take their ideas into the classroom; training at work is changing too, as teachers take their educational ideas into companies and influence staff development programmes. This will influence adult expectations of education before long.

Universities have had an increasingly influential role researching community development issues and training field workers. This role is likely to increase with government demands for more research evidence on best practices in adult education and learning. Portugal has still many serious skills shortages to address if it is to remain competitive in Europe. This cannot be solved by school reforms alone; inadequacies within the community and workplace must be tackled with urgency. While cash might come from employers, unions, the government's social partners and, increasingly, individuals, more must come from the public purse. Ministers will demand firm evidence, backed by sound research, to prove that the cash is being well spent. The universities look destined to play a strong role here, as they do at present in the training of the adult-learning enablers.

Another relatively new style of institution that is likely to emerge is the distance learning and vocational training centre. A mass transport system affordable to such diverse and isolated rural communities is out of the question; since the learner cannot go to the centre then the centre must go to the learner.

One effect of the reforms proposed in the national strategy appears to be a further blurring of the institutional boundaries in education – and the emergence of "networks" far more in tune with the community spirit of Portugal.

Case studies

Case study 1

Project: raising expectations and achievement levels among shanty dwellers.

Starting Date: 1997.

Organisation in charge: multi-agency community development partnership.

Location: Lisbon.

Community development which drew on informal adult learning programmes succeeded in raising achievement and expectations among shanty dwellers. The sense of ownership created among the people has helped make the programme and the improvements sustainable.

Overview

Many of the 16 000 people in small urban areas of Lisbon are seriously deprived migrants living in old decaying houses and shantytowns that have grown on wasteland near railways and motorways. With the communities trapped in a spiral of under-achievement, a group of mothers within the community expressed concern and asked the university faculty of social work for help. The result was the Campolide project to raise expectations by offering lessons and workshops, outside the formal education system, with emphasis on building confidence and skills.

Other problems for urban communities emerged when migrants were displaced from shantytowns in the wake of road building schemes. A 1960s social housing programme for 2 000 people in Bairro Padre Cruz has expanded dramatically, with new apartments for 8 000 migrants of mainly African and rural origin. The authorities also moved gypsies from the planned Expo 98 site to former inadequately converted army warehouses, a mile from the main bairro.

The community suffers from high unemployment and drug abuse. School is not seen as a priority by the poorly educated parents. Almost four in ten children drop out by the age of 10, rejecting the move to schools outside the community where they feel stigmatised because of their origins. A school-based project offers recurrent education to adults in an effort to increase self esteem and raise awareness of the value of education.

Two very distinctive initiatives have emerged, one focusing on the old run-down inner-city area of houses and small shops, the other in the poorer shantytowns which, while having more open space and trees around, had other problems such as those associated with a stigmatised gypsy community.

The area has specific problems of school truancy and drug abuse. The community development project was launched with a very broad set of community aims as well as specific objectives including efforts to bring the young back into the community with a sense of ownership and purpose.

Projects

Campolide

For migrants, alienation arises from the stigma of being an outsider and a loss of identity with the past, whether they be immigrants from a foreign land or migrants within. Where possible, therefore, the voluntary committee overseeing the Campolide project arranges visits to take migrants back to their communities of origin. The aim of the work is to "unlock potential" and demonstrate to participants that they have talents and histories which are valued. There are also discussions on the history of migration and issues of poverty and exclusion.

The committee draws on a range of resources and experts, including financial and legal advisers, a professional teacher for basic education, voluntary workers and students of economics and psychology on placements from university.

Project workers organise "Life Parties" to celebrate birthdays of community members born in a particular month, when others in the community make presents for them. The stress is on teamwork, a skill lacking in relatively young people who lead isolated lives. Very basic education is offered to all over 15, to raise self confidence. Marketing support is given to encourage the setting-up of small enterprises around handicrafts, cookery, information technology and dance. Adults from Cape Verde who formed an African dance group for recreation now have the confidence to give public performances. Women with an interest in cookery are studying essential basic and commercial skills to open an African restaurant. A programme based around life histories is being shaped to raise the self-esteem of Kindergarten minders who have years of experience but no formal qualifications.

Recently acquired European funding has given young people opportunities to visit Germany and Finland, to experience different cultures and offer alternative role models. It also paid for new courses in administration and computer-aided design to help develop the new enterprises.

Bairro Padre Cruz

There is not a strong sense of exclusion in the Bairro, according to the teachers involved in the community programme. Most people were in similar circumstances and had low expectations of employment and education. The biggest problems of social stigma affected the gypsy community. They were generally not reflective about their lives or circumstances. Work in the project – primarily a scheme for women returners – focuses, therefore, on raising consciousness of the potential benefits of education, which is not self-evident to many. Incentives through the Minimum Income scheme – which provides a wage to those who stick to agreed education programmes – are offered to attract adults to evening classes in recurrent education.

During the OECD visit, the strongest commitment shown was by women. All identified supporting their children as the main reason for studying. One had joined to discourage her daughter from dropping out of primary school. Another wanted the basic education needed for a driving licence. Most had themselves dropped out of school as young as 10 years old to look after siblings.

Very basic lessons in, for example, information technology skills have proved successful. But efforts by the school to run a European-funded course at a higher level failed when only nine people applied; they needed 15 under the rules of the scheme. Participation in general is low. There is a unanimous belief among those involved in the project that drug abuse is the most pressing problem facing the community. However, community discussions on current topics from drugs to sex education and AIDS attract no more than a dozen from a community of 10 000.

A community group brings together a range of agencies including the municipality, school, gypsy agency, parent's association, young people's association and the church-based charity Misericordia for monthly meetings to discuss issues and problems.

Outcomes

An overwhelming majority of the 350 people so far involved in the Campolide project have remained active, with only about 60 having lost contact. Of the remainder, one half are involved in youth and out-of-school activities, the other half are in pre-vocational learning.

Barriers to participation have emerged, including the anxiety that it might jeopardise employment in the black market or grey economy; for many, the only certain source of a living. Pressures of long and unpredictable working hours also militated against involvement for many people. Students worked up to 14 hours a day, on top of maybe running a family. Other negative influences included hostility from members of the family, which particularly affected women whose husbands resented their learning. But these issues are being addressed by the project workers and community as a whole as the project develops.

143|

In Bairro Padre Cruz, the project never reached the level of popularity that the Campolide scheme achieved. For the small group interviewed during the OECD visit, the school-based recurrent learning programmes and attendant discussions provided a basis for achieving specific goals. But the teachers agreed that, overall, very few of the wider community participated.

Two essential differences existed between the schemes. Firstly, in Campolide the project operated outside the formal education system, with which relations appear to be tolerant but not warm. The Bairro Padre Cruz programme was essentially mainstream and managed by teachers trained for children rather than adults. Despite good intentions, it is less clear that the recurrent education model works, whereas the Campolide was clearly working well on a variety of fronts.

Case study 2

Project: economic and social renewal in an isolated rural region.

Starting date: 1984.

Organisation in charge: multi-agency programme under several ministries.

Location: Sabrosa.

Investment in a sustained programme of development reversed the long-term declining economic fortunes of isolated communities. Adult learning, linked to well-targeted social policies made the projects more than the standard development programme.

Overview

Few places in Europe have been hit as hard by rural depopulation as has the isolated mountain district of Sabrosa in the Northeast. The small town of Sabrosa itself is a community of 8 000, surrounded by still more isolated communities. Agriculture declined – having always been a marginal industry – and people left to work elsewhere in Portugal and other parts of Europe. Some return annually and retain houses and farms, managed by those who remain. Most first generation migrants return eventually to settle, but more recent migrants seem less likely to do so.

Now, support from several agencies including the government, European Union, enterprising individuals and the communities themselves, has helped create rapid growth in tourism in the village. Elsewhere in the district, similar multi-agency support programmes brought significant gains in agriculture, raised educational standards and revived communities. Nowhere is this better illustrated than in the very small village of Garganta.

Projects

Sabrosa

Sabrosa boasts a hotel of international standard at the centre of a flourishing tourism industry. Traditional buildings have been restored, using skills developed by local people who benefit from the tourists which the small town attracts. At the same time, unique measures to create "relevant" adult learning programmes such as basic literacy were designed to both improve educational achievement and revive local agriculture which had been running at barely subsistence level. Basic literacy programmes were linked to giving farmers access to materials for essential improvements in tasks such as sheep-dipping.

The work that helped the growth of tourism started 14 years ago, the brainchild of a single community development worker. Backed by the community, it soon attracted support from other agencies, including the government, which earmarked this town as the location for the hotel as part of the national strategy for economic renewal.

European funding provided pre-vocational training, mainly to young people, in electrical repairs, carpentry, decorative arts and cookery. There is a problem in further developing these skills since the nearest vocational institute is 20 km away in Vila Real and public transport is poor. At the time of the OECD visit, however, the community was close to sealing a deal with the training institute to provide outreach programmes. Out of school cultural education was also funded by the Ministry of Education across an enormous range of activities, from traditional dance to sheep shearing.

A European Union-funded partnership between Sabrosa and Flanders in Belgium helped establish literacy classes. Student visits and correspondence by e-mail about the different lives and activities in the two communities helped encourage learning.

In fact, once inspired to learn and boost tourism, the community considerably exploited the opportunities for EU-funded programmes. Support has been provided to help community associations give accredited training to voluntary workers. A network of local authorities in Portugal (including Sabrosa), Belgium, Denmark and Spain has been created on the Internet to share experiences of innovations and social and professional education in rural communities. The EU New Opportunities for Women programme will pay to help 24 women in Sabrosa set up micro enterprises, giving 800 hours business education and start-up cash for those with successful business plans.

145|

Sabrosa – Garganta

A recent performance of music and drama for the President of Portugal made national newspaper headlines and attracted considerable political attention. The initiative for the one-off display of amazing talent in the tiny northern village of Garganta came from members of the community who approached the President's cook. The cook was herself from the isolated rural hamlet of just 200 people; what was achieved symbolised how a community had transformed itself in just a decade from being dependent on less than subsistence agriculture to managing its own affairs proudly and profitably.

The community development project that reshaped the village started in 1986. The local school had just 50 children, many with serious learning difficulties, and almost two-thirds of the adults were illiterate. The community association asked the Ministry of Education to help improve the children's attainment levels. With the help of staff from the University of Vila Real, who carried out a needs analysis, a series of supported self-help initiatives was taken by community development workers.

At primary school level, a parents' committee was established; it brought in specialists such as psychologists. Parents and grandparents became involved in the work of the school. They helped teachers and tought such activities as woodwork and dressmaking, thereby reinforcing their status in the eyes of children and reviving lost skills. Visits outside the village were organised, everywhere from cinema to seaside, to broaden horizons. Parents helped remodel the school, with the help of young people with pre-vocational skills gained 15 km away in Sabrosa; families also helped to landscape the school grounds.

A basic adult education programme was tailored to the needs of the community. For example, there were reading texts based on the care and husbandry of sheep – the focus of local farming. At pre-school level a playgroup was created, staffed by local young women, who were given the necessary training and professional support. Educational drama presented by outside groups spurred the community on to form their own village drama group that gave performances based on local issues.

As activities expanded, the people of Garganta realised that they needed their own community centre, and so they set about fund-raising. Support came from all over, including from people who had migrated, until they reached their Esc 50 000 target. Their latest venture is a museum of traditional skills and crafts.

Outcomes

There is evidence from the whole district that prolonged investment in community development projects, on several fronts simultaneously, not only increases resources but raises the horizons of the community. It can stabilise and even reverse rural decline. In Sabrosa, people see increased employment through tourism and real incentives to pull together and develop the rapidly expanding leisure industry. Individuals have benefited too, improving their basic literacy, obtaining wider technical and personal competences and gaining skills in new information and communication technologies.

The community of Garganta has witnessed a remarkable renewal of local pride, culminating in national acclaim and support from many who had migrated for work elsewhere. Equally remarkable are the adult education gains. After four years of programmes using tailored reading materials, there were no illiterate people over 50. Younger people who refused initially to join the courses are now signing up. Moreover, the "vocational" reading schemes have improved animal husbandry (and profitability). For more than ten years, the people relied on the outside help of a professional development worker. By the time of the OECD visit, however, a Community Association had been created, working without the need of external support.

Case study 3

The Projects: lifelong learning for economic survival.

Starting date: 1995.

Organisations in charge: community-based organisation and the company AMTROL-ALFA.

Location: Guimaraes.

1) *A very flexible approach by government agencies to the bureaucratic regulations for childminders, succeeded in drawing many older women back into the community and giving very young children a better start in life.*

2) *A work-based project in the same community provided a lifeline by helping prevent mass redundancies which could have destroyed the community.*

Overview

Guimaraes in the north is the oldest city in Portugal, with a well-established textile industry employing 70 per cent of the workforce. The city's key position on international trade routes was recently recognised by the US oil pipeline giant, AMTROL, which purchased a local family firm, Alfa. The firm is the largest manufacturer of bottled gas cylinders in the world. For the region, the industry is second in size only to textiles. Two reasons for the US company's interest were: the city's prime location for export to northern Europe, southern Africa and South America;

147

and the relatively low labour costs compared with Singapore, from where it had decided to relocate the industry.

AMTROL-ALFA is demanding new skills from workers, as is the textiles and other industries, transformed by new technology. It is not just the workers of today, however, who need retraining. An official review of education and training standards within the population revealed a need for intervention at almost every level. A series of projects, funded from a variety of sources was created by a small team of staff within the community, to help raise standards throughout the education system and create employment opportunities.

Projects

Guimaraes

Problems start in the pre-school years. Ministry of Social Solidarity rules for childminders are stringent: they must be aged 21 to 45 and adhere to strict controls in the facilities they provide. Many families cannot afford the provision and place their children with older women who lack training and operate from home, outside the legal framework. As a result, children from poorer families enter school ill-prepared, leaving them more prone to failure and drop-out.

Ser Criança ("to be a child") is a response to the problem. Research through community leaders identified 46 women caring for 112 children through the black market economy. They were visited by project staff who offered advice, professional training and playgroup resources for the home, which they accepted once reassured that it would not threaten their precarious legal status with the Ministry. From this has grown a basic education programme for the childminders who now have the resources of a well-equipped community association building. An innovative feature is the combination of individualised, home-based tuition and regular group sessions away from home.

Another study revealed the extent to which earlier cycles of under-achievement had blighted young lives. A survey showed that at least 500 young people in a medium-sized community of 17 000 had not completed nine years of schooling. Project workers contacted 100 of these with offers of training, under a programme of "tailored personal and vocational development". Fifty accepted and were given core skills and basic education followed by a choice of pre-vocational training in electrical studies, secretarial work, motor mechanics and childcare.

The same project team offered people with enterprising ideas a chance to start their own small companies, backed by a mixture of formal and pre-vocational education plus guidance in drafting a business plan. As in the earlier Sabrosa scheme, if successful, they were offered "start-up" support for a micro enterprise. The encouragement of small to medium-sized enterprises has grown significantly in Portugal; the *Formacao* PME (SME enterprise training) was set up to help the process.

The fourth main strand to the Guimaraes community development programme is support for the older long-term unemployed, through a European-funded scheme, to re-equip them with work and social skills. The scheme, that starts with a three-month education programme, has four aims:

- occupational and educational guidance;
- development of self esteem;
- citizenship skills and knowledge;
- visits to workplaces.

Community development staff have helped create an annual fair of local crafts. This has resulted in increased local pride and provided an outlet for many of the products of enterprises started by those on the various schemes.

Guimaraes – Alfa

The establishment of AMTROL-ALFA as a leading employer in Guimaraes brought a range of education and training opportunities. The firm, employing 750 local workers, had relocated its plant for producing disposable gas cylinders from Singapore to Portugal to cut world export and labour costs. In the medium term, the plan is to switch less specialist work to elsewhere, leaving the Portuguese plant with more specialised high-skill demands, provided the workforce is available. The company operates in a field where health and safety issues are paramount. Managers are concerned about the low educational levels among workers, a significant number of whom were with the old family firm for many years.

The company expressed a wish to help individual staff with human resource development and show its belief in the importance of building loyalty and commitment towards the regional community. A range of courses was offered to staff at all levels, from basic literacy to management and technical training. Help was given towards the costs of transport and materials for any worker wishing to attend classes, under a basic education teacher, which were financed by the EU and government.

Time off was granted to all staff who committed themselves to the same number of hours, which were considered necessary to complete private study. Courses are popular among staff of all ages, from their teens to their sixties. Many adults had finished primary education and had not kept up their literacy skills, and so additional support was given here too. The company provides over 4 000 hours management training a year. The whole project is supported by the trade unions which are said to have very good relations with the firm. Staff interviewed during the OECD visit said they were in favour of the programmes and attended because the employers encouraged them. For some, this was despite difficulties fitting studies around night shifts.

149|

Outcomes

In Guimaraes, a multi-stranded body of work was helping overcome exclusion of older women who had been educationally excluded since childhood. Their return to learning is helping change the expectations of the next generation. It was not just the range of informal learning opportunities that mattered, it was the willingness of the authorities to recognise the limitations of policies (which had been drawn up with the best intentions for children) and to be flexible when interpreting the regulations.

The work at AMTROL-ALFA although very new, was clearly bringing people from the margins of the workforce into a community where their employment prospects, and self respect were being raised. Tangible educational benefits came to many, including one woman in her 60s who learned to read. Another was determined to read in defiance of her husband's objections, a familiar cry from Portuguese women in the OECD case studies.

It is an innovative area of involvement for an employer. But it raises further questions about longer-term arrangements: whether the workers will have gained the skills needed when the switch of low-skill tasks to Eastern Europe comes. If not, how secure is the future of the plant in the longer term?

Innovation and effectiveness

Four issues among many stand out in the Portugal case studies:

- The Campolide project was innovative in building a diverse range of initiatives outside the formal education and training system. Jobs were created within an increasingly self-confident community. The initiative lasts because the community owns it, not the state.

- Sabrosa town was effective in galvanising various sources of cash and original ideas to develop agriculture and tourism. In doing so, they revived traditional skills and a whole community.

- Few could boast the success of the small village (200 people) of Garganta in being commissioned to perform before the President. Theirs is a unique model of small-scale, long-term investment for sustainability and self-sufficiency.

- The Guimaraes community was innovative in the extreme in asking the government to take a more flexible attitude to unofficial child-minding, for those who pledged to take proper training. In promoting education for all, the initiative broke the spiral of under-achievement in the early school years and, early indications suggest, throughout life.

Commentary

Portugal is undergoing dramatic change as a society, including rapid transformation of its education for adults. It starts with great strengths in terms of people and pockets of very good practice. But the challenges are formidable, with an estimated one-third of the population currently excluded, a figure which could grow as economic competition increases. The national strategy seeks to address the problem, and its proposals seem well judged, as does the approach to implementation through widespread consultation. If Portugal can build a structure which draws on the leading edge skills and talents which it has, it stands a good chance of meeting the challenge.

There are students with the calibre and commitment to succeed, regardless of low levels of educational achievement. Parents share a concern that their children should have better opportunities than they themselves had. Those pursuing basic education share a sense of having been liberated from serious exclusion.

A considerable strength is the integrated approach, combining staff from several ministries and community organisations, with funds from many sources, including significant sums from the EU. The policy, which will be taken much further under the national strategy, was very effective: educating older women who care for the children of poorer people pays in raised expectations in the next generation; providing pre-vocational skills to young people makes it possible to carry out building improvements at manageable cost; encouraging the maintenance of traditional skills raises the self-confidence and self-esteem of individuals and communities alike.

The commitment and skills of key staff – especially the local team members – was crucial. However, teams are appointed on one-year contracts and no formal qualifications exist for this role. These factors militate against continuity and professional development, although some staff are very committed and the typical member has been in post for ten years.

In Sabrosa and Guimaraes, local authorities are significant players in community development and education to overcome exclusion, particularly in providing well-equipped buildings. Staff at this level are clear about the importance of combining bottom-up and top-down approaches to planning, about the need for partnerships which balance the rights of all parties, and about building on the strengths of individuals and communities. There is clear success in using educational resources to recognise the value, and maintain the continuation of traditional skills and crafts, and to use these as the basis for small scale economic activity.

As one worker said – "the project is part of the community, the community is not considered as just a target group; our job is to create the belief that change is possible".

151|

UNITED KINGDOM

Sunderland

Dudley

London

Total population (1996): 58 782 000
– age structure of population 15-64
  (1996): 64.9%;
– age structure of population 65 and over
  (1996): 15.7%.

Land size area: 245 000 sq km.

Per capita GDP (1996 prices): US$19 621.

Annual percentage growth rate (1997): 3.3%.

1997 unemployment rate: 7.1%:
– proportion unemployed for 12 months or
  more: 38.6%.

**Expenditure on education per student
(1995):** US$4 222.

**Percentage of population aged 25-64 with
at least upper secondary education:** 76%.

Sources: OECD (1998*h*), *Employment Outlook*;
"OECD in Figures – 1998"; OECD (1998*g*),
Education at a Glance.

"The thing about Return to Learn is that it really made me think about the wider world. It made me just a little bit more aware, and then a little bit more interested in why things happen, and then of course I wanted to start interfering myself. I got stuck into the UNISON (trade union) branch, helping other people out if they had trouble, and giving a bit of encouragement to other people if they were doing courses, that sort of thing. After I retired, there was the tenants and residents association; well, I knew about committees and meetings, didn't I? So it just seemed natural to get involved in that too."

After working 23 years as a hospital cleaner, this learner retired and became secretary of her local residents' association. A college created by her union gave learning opportunities for greater involvement in work and retirement.

Note: While the data above are for United Kingdom as a whole, the following study is limited to England (the area shaded in the map).

United Kingdom (England)

Context

Britain is widely viewed as the cradle of the industrial revolution. Such thinking still exerts a powerful influence over the nation. Yet, where coal mining alone once employed more than 250 000 workers – creating the wealth to feed, clothe and house 6 million people – by the mid-1990s, all the mining and quarrying activities combined accounted for just 0.5 per cent of the workforce. Memories of the revolution may still have a strong resonance, but it is increasingly symbolic. Coal mines and factories are parts of a national heritage; miners and weavers now serve as tourist guides.

The symbolism of earlier industrial dominance was evoked in the government's 1998 Green Paper on lifelong learning, *The Learning Age*, in order to highlight the scale of today's challenges: "The Industrial Revolution was built on capital investment in plant and machinery, skills and hard physical labour. British inventors pushed forward the frontiers of technology and our manufacturers turned their inventions into wealth. Our history shows what we are capable of, but we must now apply the same qualities of skill and invention to a fresh challenge. The information and knowledge-based revolution of the 21st century will be built on a very different foundation – investment in the intellect and creativity of people."

The information revolution has already brought significant change to employment patterns in the UK: it contributed to the sharp decline in manufacturing which had begun in the 1970s, while new jobs have been predominantly in the service sectors. Part-time and fixed-term employment are now of considerable significance, as is self-employment and the creation of small-scale firms and even micro-enterprises. In ten years from 1986, as OECD figures show, the number of men in part-time jobs almost doubled from 4.6 to 8.1 per cent of the male workforce, while male unemployment rates fell from 13.5 to 9.7 per cent. In the same period, unemployment rates for women fell from 8.9 to 6.3 per cent. Decline in unemployment has not been reflected in levels of economic growth. Out of all 29 OECD countries in 1998, the UK recorded the fifth lowest growth in GDP for 1998 at just 1.7 per cent.

155|

The UK is a large and diverse society combining four national areas (England, Scotland, Wales and Northern Ireland). The present report is concerned primarily with England which has around 49 million people out of a UK total population of 58.6 million; 7 million (14 per cent) living in the capital city, London.

By global standards, England is a relatively elderly country with increasingly profound implications for health and welfare costs. The under-16s account for just one in five of the population (compared with one in four in Ireland, for example), while almost one in six is over 65 and 2 million are over 80.

Participation in post-compulsory education and training has expanded rapidly: the proportion of young people going into higher education, for example, rose from just 20 per cent in the late 1980s to 32 per cent in 1996. Reasons are many: they reflect high levels of youth unemployment, recognition of the demand for higher skills, qualifications inflation and the disappearance of well-paid low-skill work with the rise of information technology.

The information revolution is still in its early stages. As an established capital-ist economy, the UK now faces new competitive pressures. Globalising tendencies, rapid technical change, restructuring and the communications revolution have prompted a demand for flexibility and high added-value products. The cognitive and technical capacities of the workforce have therefore become a major political issue. Politicians and policy makers have only recently begun to address in depth how adult education meets the challenges. In the UK, the term "social exclusion" is only just becoming widely recognised. "Poverty" rather than "social exclusion" is the term that sets the agenda for policy and research. It is the former term also which still dominates public discourse about the gap between the "haves" and "have-nots" in the context of debates about the best ways of creating a learning society.

Problems of exclusion in the United Kingdom

Despite recently falling unemployment in the 1990s, there has been a spread of precarious and poorly-paid jobs. This has added to the growing polarisation between the affluent majority and disadvantaged, a trend that started in the late 1970s. The risks of increased social exclusion have been recognised, and the incom-ing government in 1997 accepted that it had inherited a situation of growing welfare dependency and increasing deprivation in some sections of society.

The evidence in England is that while society as a whole has become more affluent, the position of the poorest has become worse, in relative if not absolute terms. Most indicators used for assessing poverty underline this trend. A more com-prehensive view of social exclusion is being taken by the government, but poverty indicators are still considered the most important measure. Researchers at Oxford

University in 1997 studied how much family income remained after housing costs were deducted. In 1971, just 7 per cent of homes fell below the poverty line; by 1990 a quarter, did so. Research for the Joseph Rowntree Charitable Trust, also in 1997, suggested this is a peculiarly British trend. The study showed that the proportion of UK households with an income of less than half the national average was double that found in Belgium Denmark, Finland, Italy, and the Netherlands.

Exclusion also affects some localities more than others. The Townsend Deprivation Index, based on car-ownership, home-ownership, over-crowding, security and unemployment, shows enormous variations between such areas of multiple deprivation as Inner London, Tyneside and Merseyside and the lowest ranked districts such as the south east of England and the M4 corridor. Big regional variations are indicated in the International Labour Organisation's 1996 employment data which shows pockets of new affluence in the south (unemployment at 6 per cent in London) and continued deprivation in the north (Merseyside: 13.3 per cent).

For those who are unemployed, the further threat of social and domestic isolation remains. The OECD *Employment Outlook* report of 1998 shows that over half of those out of work in the UK live in households where no one has a job. This is one of the highest rates recorded in OECD countries

Wealth is not the only yardstick of exclusion; there is a question of the social capital people possess. That includes access to networks, civic engagement and membership of associations. Recent studies of political participation in the UK show that the middle class is much more likely to become involved than is the working class; middle class people also join more clubs and associations. This means that those most vulnerable to exclusion are increasingly less able to call upon social-support networks.

Groups disproportionately at risk of exclusion in the UK include ex-offenders, the homeless, those with special educational needs and the unskilled. A survey of large-scale employers by a London training and enterprise council in 1997, found that seven out of ten people would not offer a job to a homeless person or to someone with a criminal record. Three out of ten managers interviewed said they would not consider recruiting a young person who lacked formal qualifications.

Poor levels of literacy, from which such groups suffer disproportionately, are also a factor. The OECD's International Adult Literacy Study showed that in 1995, average unemployment rates among those with the lowest two levels of proficiency were 17.5 per cent, as against 7.7 per cent for those with the top three levels (see OECD and Statistics Canada, 1995 and 1997).

Participation in lifelong learning is a factor in determining social exclusion, as shown by two recent surveys of adult learning. One was by the National Institute for Adult Continuing Education (NIACE) in 1996, the other in 1997 was from the Department for Education and Employment. Profiles of non-learners in both were: women (much more likely than men to reject learning); older adults; people without paid work; those who were caring for children or other relatives at home; manual workers, people with disability or illness and those who left school young and with no qualifications. Half of the non-learners in the 1997 study said there was nothing that would change their lack of interest in learning.

Another 1996 study for NIACE suggested that unsuccessful participation was often worse than not attempting to learn. Four groups identified as most likely to withdraw early from a course were: the unemployed; those with low incomes and other financial problems; minority ethnic groups; and, in some subject areas, men. For such groups, there was a big risk that returning to learn would reinforce earlier experiences of failure.

Educational disadvantage is not always a factor in exclusion. A study of welfare claimants between 1992 and 1994 showed that many – particularly the unemployed and lone parents – suffered little or no educational disadvantage. Ill health was a common feature among claimants in the survey. This suggests that active labour market strategies are needed alongside other measures to tackle multiple causes of exclusion.

As policy analysis looks beyond income as the single factor causing exclusion, there is better appreciation of the influence poor initial education and training can have. This has influenced the debate on standards in schools and led to some highly innovative schemes where initial education is, as it should be, a part of life-long learning (case study No. 2).

Adult learning and social exclusion

Government plans to reform education in England and Wales were published in a 1972 White Paper: "Education: A Framework for Expansion." Three years later, an OECD review of policies pointed to a central weakness: the paper had totally ignored adult education. At the end of the 1970s, the political focus was still almost entirely on school reforms, following the great debate on the failure of schools to prepare people for adult life. The question of educational supply to minority groups – addressing aspects of social exclusion that went wider than those of employment – was scarcely on the political agenda.

Government adult education policies throughout the 1980s and early 1990s, promoted a strong reliance on the market. Skills training for the unemployed was high on the policy agenda and a network of 81 training and enterprise councils was set up to channel government grants into meeting local skills shortages and schemes to encourage enterprise. While the encouragement of enterprise was meant to be the main task of TECs, their role through the early 1990s was increasingly as overseers of job creation schemes and private training providers' initiatives for jobless young adults. There was virtually no role for general adult education in combating unemployment and fostering competitivity. The non-vocational and recreational adult education that did exist had much of its public funding removed under the 1992 Further and Higher Education Act.

A wider range of initiatives to tackle exclusion in the 1980s was stimulated or supported by local government, trade unions, employers or voluntary and community organisations (case study No. 3). Historically, the labour movement has been a very big provider of adult education. Institutions of world renown, such as Ruskin College, Oxford, and the Northern College in Barnsley, were products of the thinkers in the wider movement around the turn of the last century.

Industry too has had an historic role creating guilds responsible for training and the personal development of apprentices. With the rapid decline in traditional apprenticeships in the 1970s and 1980s, that has waned. But many large companies are re-emerging with education development plans to rank alongside the colleges and universities. There was a rapid spread of schemes, building on the success of the Employee Development Assistance Programme at Ford UK in 1987 which achieved an unexpectedly high participation rate of well over 30 per cent a year. Most participants had no previous involvement in continuing education. Schemes, usually supported by the trade unions, offered financial help and time off to employees who took general education or job-related learning. Often targeted at non-participant groups, the schemes included a significant return-to-learn dimension. Employee development programmes were particularly attractive to shift-workers who were unable to attend a regularly scheduled class. Above all, they benefit employees faced with job restructuring or redundancy.

Adult education providers such as Ford and TEC-funded organisations, tackling social exclusion, needed a means of accrediting a rapidly growing range of adult learning programmes. The Open College Networks (OCNs) were created in the late 1980s to assess work, moderate programmes and often give credits towards nationally-recognised qualifications. By 1998 some 28 OCNs in England were being used by 2 100 providers, including 580 voluntary organisations, 450 further education colleges, employers, private training providers and adult education centres. Between 1993 and 1996, OCN registrations rose from 90 000 to 355 000, the number of credits awarded went from 353 000 to 930 000. A study in 1998 by the National Open College Network estimated that 18 per cent of people on OCN-accredited courses were unemployed, 12 per cent were part-time employed and 62 per cent were women; 16 per cent were from the ethnic minorities and 8 per cent had additional learning needs. Through the OCNs, providers of the adult learning levered funds, for marginalised and vulnerable groups, from bodies ranging from charitable trusts and foundations to government funding agencies.

159

Main policy approaches

By the mid-1990s, Britain was still some way from becoming a learning society. In 1991, the government endorsed national targets for education and training which had been drafted by the Confederation of British Industry and backed by the Trades Union Congress. Three lifetime learning targets were aimed at improving vocational and professional skills in the workforce and in getting companies to invest in equipping employees with new skills and competencies. By the mid-1990s, lifetime learning was viewed as something which promoted individual advancement and corporate and national competitivity; its role in respect of social inclusion was limited and largely remedial action.

Little reference was made to disadvantaged or excluded groups in government recommendations on lifelong learning. Nor did a subsequent policy consultation around lifetime learning lead to any significant new departures; rather, it strengthened the definition as chiefly to do with the retraining adults in job-specific skills.

Compared with other European nations, there has been little emphasis in the UK on negotiation between the social partners to boost competitivity and growth. Rather, policy has been to cut costs through deregulation and privatisation. Welfare and job-creation measures were used in the 1980s and most of the 1990s for the continued management by TECs of high unemployment levels.

European social legislation in 1997 coincided with the election of a new Labour government which pledged to tackle social exclusion. Early challenges identified by ministers included: making lifelong learning a reality; helping dependent people move from welfare to work; tackling deprivation and social exclusion; and creating a fair and flexible labour market. Wider collaboration with the social partners such as the CBI and TUC was also promised.

The 1998 Green Paper on Lifelong Learning proposed three significant new initiatives. Firstly a national free-phone helpline would be available for information and advice on learning opportunities. Secondly, a University for Industry (UfI) would be created to find new ways of providing learning opportunities. The UfI is not intended to be a provider but a broker, issuing contracts for research into market needs and to commission the design of courses which would be provided wherever they were needed. That might be the home, workplace, shopping mall or sports ground. Methods of reaching under-achievers with low-cost learning programmes are currently on trial in a North East England pilot scheme (case study No. 1) Thirdly, Individual Learning Accounts, financed by individuals and employers with support from the government, would be created to help people pay the costs of new opportunities.

In 1998, the government introduced the "New Deal" to help young people remain competitive within the labour market. Welfare benefits were tied to a limited range of options for young unemployed under 25, and later for older people, who were offered a combination of training and work experience or education with the aim of enhancing employability and giving access to vocational qualifications. Government also called for a change in attitudes towards education and training, as deep cynicism towards job creation schemes had developed among young people who had seen a succession of youth schemes fail. In preparing for the introduction of the New Deal, the London TEC Council reported that young people were frequently sceptical about the value of training programmes, which they saw as demeaning and not leading to a "proper job".

The United Kingdom still has a tremendous challenge encouraging more men from manual backgrounds into adult learning. A significant, resistant minority of women are also refusers. Both are particularly at risk of exclusion and long-term unemployment.

There is also still the need for the UK to understand social exclusion more clearly in terms other than the job market. A school-based community project in Dudley (case study No. 2) illustrates how inclusive projects can raise self-esteem and revive communities, regardless of job creation.

It is important to note that the wider debate is not limited to lifelong learning for employment. The Commission on Social Justice took a strong view on the importance of an inclusive sense of community. Drawing on the work of the American political scientist Robert Putnam, the Commission called for a greater willingness to invest in "social capital" – those networks, norms and trust that promote co-ordination and co-operation between citizens and organisations in pursuing common goals.

Case studies

Case study 1

Project: to pilot a new University for Industry and reach socially excluded minorities.

Starting date: 1997.

Organisation in charge: partnership of industry, community groups education and training providers and the government.

Location: Sunderland, north east England.

More than 4 000 adults, including the retired, sick and long-term unemployed, in a depressed region of England, overcame their fear of learning on a project that was nationally-acclaimed as a model for people facing social exclusion.

Overview

Sunderland has been a city in decline for 70 years. Like much of north-east England, it suffered disproportionately from de-industrialisation and geographical

161

isolation. Heavy engineering, the region's economic lifeblood, has been in continuous decline since the 1920s. The 1936 march of unemployed demonstrators from nearby Jarrow to London symbolised, for generations of Britons, the human damage wrought by the depression of the interwar years.

Recovery began recently, led partly by the Japanese automotive manufacturer Nissan's decision to site its UK assembly plant just outside the city. The service sector has grown too, though offering largely low-wage, part-time jobs. Yet, on the various UK poverty indices, Sunderland still comes between 29th and ninth from the bottom out of 366 districts. In the early 1990s, the city gained national notoriety for crime and record levels of theft from cars.

However, Sunderland was fortunate in one respect: many of the leading partners in government-backed urban regeneration programmes lived and worked there. The economic slump of the late 1980s brought many small to medium enterprises to bankruptcy; renewal was urgently needed. More than half the workforce is self employed or working in small companies. Failure of firms to recover quickly in the 1990s was blamed in part on the lack of accessible, affordable packages to retrain the workforce, particularly middle managers, many of whom faced the unthinkable prospect of long-term unemployment. Companies needed new skills of the information and communication technologies for full recovery.

Sunderland was chosen in 1997 for a project to widen participation in adult learning – a scheme foreshadowing the national launch of a University for Industry. The pilot project, like the UfI itself, was to be a "broker and catalyst" rather than provider of adult education and training courses. It was created to attract learners from disaffected groups and marginalised backgrounds and to identify providers who could best meet their needs.

Ideas for the UfI were developed by the Institute for Public Policy Research (IPPR), a politically left-leaning think-tank; a blueprint was published in 1996 for a "university" that would raise public awareness of education and training opportunities at further education colleges, universities, distance learning centres and industry training centres. The next step was to connect individuals and companies to learning programmes. Subsequently the IPPR and the University of Sunderland developed proposals for a pilot project in north-eastern England to test out the ideas.

Projects

The Sunderland scheme caught the media's imagination from the start, with a launch at Sunderland Football Club's stadium and announcements of colourfully described courses such as IT for the Terrified. A powerful partnership of local authorities, Sunderland College, the university, a government-backed training and enterprise council and leading figures in sports and the arts were involved. Funding came from big businesses and banks. They caught the public imagination largely by the way they took the courses to the people. Almost anywhere was seen as a potential learning centre: pubs, clubs, community centres, works canteens.

Courses and learning programmes were tailor-made and available immediately in small chunks or units to those who wanted them. Project organisers rapidly discovered that would-be learners, particularly those who were nervous about returning to learn, did not want long-term commitments; they wanted short courses right away. A well-publicised freephone advice and guidance service was made available. Taster courses across wide-ranging interests included Internet for All, All about Football, Telephone Skills and Customer Care. Work packs were written in accessible language with an element of self-assessment to reduce the intimidation of external judgement and increase self-confidence. Taster courses were particularly innovative, based on a readily available mixture of 30 to 40-page work packs and tutorial support, backed up by access to IT. Every opportunity was taken for promotion: on World Book Day the project team obtained TV coverage of young people on a literacy course rehearsing Shakespeare in a Jarrow pub.

A recruitment target of 5 000 learners was set. Brochures described the project as "essentially an open-all-hours one-stop-shop for education and training". The UfI project would provide: a freephone, database, Internet link and call centre for advice and courses; a network of 35 learning centres everywhere, from libraries, schools and colleges to a cybercafé; free taster courses with help telephone help from tutors.

In addition, the UfI pilot devotes considerable energy to marketing the idea of lifelong learning to the people of the region. The organisers and main stakeholders in the project have a history of collaborating on local schemes, including imaginative ventures such as the highly-regarded Learning World, an open-access learning centre at Europe's biggest shopping mall in nearby Gateshead. They were also organising national activities such as Adult Learners' Week. By November 1997, more than 40 organisations were involved in the pilot project.

All publicity is geared towards a very simple and often-repeated message: the UfI service costs nothing, it is an easy-to-use one-stop-shop where consumers can try a range of services before making a purchase. Behind this message, though, lies a concern with far broader cultural change. The Sunderland project director said: "We're trying to get people who haven't done it in the past to realise that they can learn, and that they can achieve, and we're looking for lots of different hooks that will bring people in."

Outcomes

By May 1998, a month from the target deadline, the project had recruited 4 300 learners, 700 off target. But targets and performance were hard to monitor precisely, given the highly experimental methods of recruitment. Collection and analysis of detailed participant data was not a short term priority. Analysis of the first 1 700 to register on a taster or full course showed that 908 were women and 798 men; 315 described themselves as registered unemployed, 642 as in paid employment, and 863 as retired, working in the home, sick, injured or students.

Some groups remain largely outside the UfI pilot's reach. The partners themselves acknowledge that they have not targeted those with basic skills needs. However, the project has stimulated unanticipated demand; for example, among oil rig workers and occupational travellers.

One way in which the UfI pilot has helped to widen participation is by providing ready and effective access to information. The freephone line is widely used, often by would-be learners who are hesitant and uncertain about their eligibility to take part in any form of education or training. One guidance worker gave the example of older adults:

"People will call and if they're over sixty they'll say to you, 'Am I too old?' They are absolutely serious, they think that if they are over sixty then it cannot be for them. If they say that, you tell them "Of course you're not – we've got people registered of eighty and over, so you can't be too old". And we have had people ring up who say 'Do you have to be working to do it?'. People ring who are worried about the level of courses, the rest of it. And there are people who wouldn't ring up, even a freephone number is threatening. If we can identify a particular group, like the people who use the women's centre, we do a personal visit there."

Two problems anticipated during planning turned out to be relatively unimportant. One, was cost: although providers believed that demand was highly price elastic, the project manager had not received one complaint on the level of fees. While some learners had opted to take only the free taster courses, the majority were willing to pay. The second was content. It was expected that a large untapped demand for subjects that were unavailable would be discovered; this was not so. Rather, would-be learners wanted only those parts of the course that interested them, and they wanted them right away rather than in the following autumn.

Many learners have commented on how the initiative had changed their lives. For example, Mike was in his early thirties and feeling himself still marked by school failure. Unemployed, he found occasional work in the catering industry. Being a loyal, enthusiastic Sunderland supporter, he became part of a group from the club who were familiarising themselves with online technologies. Starting with what he described as "ignorance and terror", he had progressed to navigating the World Wide Web. "I still stand in awe of this thing, but I am starting to get somewhere". He had embarked on this journey partly out of curiosity ("I just wanted to look up the football sites and see what they had to offer") and partly out of a sense that he was missing out ("If you want to work, you're up against the young ones who have been doing this since they were knee high"). He planned to move on to a word processing course at a local college.

Having a network of influential stakeholders and organisers involved was particularly effective in bringing in extra resources. The involvement of businesses such as NatWest bank and British Telecom provided a lever. A number of other private and public sector partners provided varying levels of in-kind support, such as workbooks and software.

Inevitably, the project faces difficulties and problems. More needs to be done to widen participation among adults with basic literacy or learning needs. The project has succeeded in generating short term funding, but money is also needed for longer-term planning and innovation.

Case study 2

Project: using adult support at Priory Primary School to build a community development programme.

Starting date: 1993.

Organisation in charge: priory Primary School.

Location: Dudley, in the Midlands.

A large and socially isolated housing estate was turned into a learning community, boosting the people's sense of purpose and self-esteem. The project was an award-winning scheme that turned a primary school into a community education centre.

Overview

The West Midland conurbation of Dudley is classic middle England. It has neither the abject poverty of the North East, not the affluence of the South. Taken as a whole, it is well-placed with respect to national and international communications networks; employment is mixed, with an above-average proportion of the workforce employed in the manufacturing industries. Analysis of the 1991 population census placed Dudley 116th out of 366 districts on the Townsend Deprivation Index.

Nevertheless, as in many urban areas, parts of Dudley are less favoured than others. Priory estate is an area of council-rented houses, built between the two world wars and is a typical example. Unemployment in the local primary school's catchment area is 23 per cent, with four-fifths of those out of work being long-term unemployed. More than four out of ten pupils receive free school meals – the proxy in estimating family poverty – well above the national average. A school

165

inspectors' report in 1997 said there was a "large number of pupils who present serious short-term problems created by coming from a multi-disadvantaged background." In addition, out of 657 pupils, 209 were on the register of special educational needs.

Parents spoke vividly of their anger over the way their estate was portrayed to outsiders. Some believed that, right up to the recent past, this negative image had influenced teachers at the school. One resident, who had attended the school in the early 1950s, said: "It is like the way they talk about racial discrimination or religious discrimination today, the way the teachers treated you then if you came from one of those council houses". Participation in education and training by local adults is reportedly low; in one local survey, three-quarters of the respondents expressed no interest in improving or acquiring skills through training.

In 1993, under a new headteacher, the school decided to launch the Priory Partnership Project to raise pupil achievement by involving parents and the community. The aim was not to educate adults as such, but to use the support of parents to trigger a sharp rise in standards of literacy and numeracy and improve core academic skills among pupils. Efforts were made to raise the standards and levels of achievements among children, and to challenge parents' low self-esteem and expectations.

Those expectations were rapidly surpassed and an innovative and highly challenging adult community education programme was born. It would go on to win national acclaim.

Projects

When the Priory Primary School project began in 1993, its aims were modest: parents were asked to hear children read and to help out in the library. It was hoped that the presence of adults other than teachers around the school would motivate children and, in so doing, break the cycle of low achievement. Before long, however, the parents found themselves being encouraged and assessed by the school. Skills, competencies and achievements gained in the volunteer programme were recorded. Tutors from nearby Bilston Community College, a further and higher education institution, were brought in as moderators and before long they were presenting parents with certificates in lifelong learning.

The certificates proved to be a source of pride that spurred the parents on. Other activities developed, formal adult education programmes were created, informal clubs and interest groups emerged. Soon, a range of awards was being made. In 1995, 108 parents gained Access to Lifelong Learning certificates; by 1997 the number of awards had reached 276.

The range of programmes became increasingly sophisticated; as well as the library volunteer club there was a pre-school parent-support group, the Pop-in Club for learning basic computer skills, Family Maths and the Helping Hands Club where parenting skills were taught. College-moderated assessments were sent to the local Open College Network which issued certificates, giving the courses nationally-recognised status.

Activities at the school became a re-entry-to-learning point for parents whose own initial educational achievements were low. Staff at the school described the process as "concealed learning"; once engaged in a group, parents were actively encouraged to collect evidence of their achievements. They were asked to present the evidence in whatever form suited them best – written, tape-recorded, photographic – and the college tutor was assigned to assess their portfolios.

Since the focus of the adults' activities was all related, directly or indirectly, to their children's education, there was relevance and applicability that is often missing in more theoretical or decontextualised learning programmes. The strategic site of the primary school also opened-up a range of possibilities for using the education system more widely, in ways that are not always possible for community groups outside the world of education.

The Priory Partnership Project had considerable backing from the local education authority, the Bilston Community College, the Open College Network of the West Midlands, the school, local industry, the government-backed training and enterprise council (TEC) and the community. As the project grew, so did the parents' feelings of confidence; they embarked on a major research programme, looking at the history of the school that originally stood on the site; they invited local archaeologists to speak at discussion groups.

The history project grew so large, it became a book which will be published in the year 2000. The history research group comprises 18 parents who are looking now not just at the school but at the whole community, trawling newspaper and local council archives for evidence.

Eventually, the school became a recognised adult education centre, making it a community school in the fullest sense. National awards followed.

Outcomes

By mid-1998, 621 parents – mainly young mothers – had been awarded Open College Network certificates in lifelong learning and a number had gone on to undertake more formal courses of education and training.

A typical example was Sally – married with three children – who returned to education after volunteering to work in Priory Primary School library. When the library introduced CD-ROMs, she had to find out how they worked in order to guide the children. She then completed a course in computing, before embarking on a Second Chance to Learn course at a local college. She was subsequently elected as a parent representative on the school governing body. Her confidence had snow-balled: "Once you can see you can do things you couldn't do before, you can talk to teachers in their own language, that's when you start to see you are doing things for yourself."

She was a mature student at the University of Wolverhampton, in her third and final year of a degree in English and Education at the time of the OECD visit. She chaired the finance sub-committee of the school governing body and hopes to become a schoolteacher.

During the 1995 Adult Learner's Week, Priory became the first primary school in England to gain the Group Learners' Award for the work it had done with parents. Two years later, on the nomination of the local training and enterprise council, Priory School was awarded a National Training Award (NTA), and in 1998 it was presented with a Supreme Winner NTA.

Most of all, the project helped raise self-esteem in a community whose people had felt themselves stigmatised. Evidence of this emerged in a TEC survey of community needs in the light of the partnership project. It found that community and individual benefits came in equal measure from the work. Continued success depended on a number of factors: maintaining the partnership, giving the community control over further developments, keeping down the fees for formal adult education programmes and offering a wide range of free taster courses for potential recruits. The best form of recruitment proved to be word of mouth from friends and relatives.

Case study 3

Project: to equip adult workers with skills to prevent exclusion at work and in daily life.

Starting date: 1994.

Organisation in charge: UNISON (the largest public sector trade union).

Location: throughout the United Kingdom.

Excluded and vulnerable workers in the rapidly changing public service industries gained the social skills and confidence to improve their lives through the efforts of a new-style Open College run by their union. Many gained promotion, new jobs; all found new social and learning opportunities outside work.

Overview

Efforts to improve the education and training of many employees in the UK have too often failed due to hostility or distrust between the unions and employers. For two decades, the unions have been marginalised in negotiations between employers, staff and government aimed at bringing changes in conditions of service, usually involving considerable numbers of job losses. Some big employers created occupational and general education opportunities for their staff during the 1980s, but they were the exception, not the rule. One of the best publicised was the Ford UK Employee Development and Assistance Programme, launched in 1987. The resources committed and the number of students recruited from the shop-floor were equal to those of a medium-sized further education college or university.

The unions too have committed greater resources to education and training, but their efforts have focused more on trade union study courses and training programmes for officials. It is unusual for a trade union to choose to devote significant resources to education for its rank and file members. In 1994, however, the UK's biggest public sector union UNISON decided that action was needed to improve the prospects of members, particularly for those whose jobs were disappearing and who lacked the levels of formal education needed for redeployment. The UNISON Open College was launched to provide the union's members with courses ranging from literacy and basic skills training to degree-level studies. UNISON's membership covers a wide range of occupations, from refuse collectors to senior hospital staff; from manual and part-time staff to personnel managers. Members include a significant number of low-paid workers, many of whom have poor formal educational qualifications.

Formed from a merger of the National Union of Public Employees, the National Association of Local Government Officers and the Confederation of Health Sector Employees, UNISON inherited three separate educational departments with differing approaches to the education and training of officers and members. The UNISON Open College was launched to co-ordinate and deliver opportunities to members, drawing on the long history of trade union education as well as on more recent developments in training and adult education to promote lifelong learning. The term "college" here applies not to a traditional institution but a network of learning opportunities at work, in some institutions, and at home using distance learning.

Projects

The flagship of the Unison Open College is the Return to Learn (RTL) programme which aims to build confidence and a wide range of skills for daily life and for work. The course offers a mixture of small study groups, meeting fortnightly with tutorial support; self-study workbooks; written assignments; and occasional larger regional meetings, usually residential. Courses are free and members are given help with child care and travel costs. Tutors come from the local educational partners, usually the Workers' Educational Association which has agreed to appoint a full-time regional co-ordinator in every area where the union can recruit 80 RTL students.

Courses are specifically designed, using language and materials that are relevant to the fields encompassed by the union's activities and the occupations of its members. This ensures that the work is well grounded in useful knowledge. There are also well-structured pathways of progression from one level to the next. Since there is no fixed institutional location for learning, courses can be community-based or work-based.

Partnership is crucial. Many courses are now offered jointly with employers who agree to give each student 60 hours paid leave for study. By 1998, UNISON had signed agreements with 100 employers, who agreed also to pay all the tuition fees. Such partnerships have allowed the college to expand its RTL programme, enabling health care assistants to upgrade their qualifications and to become registered nurses. Home care staff can also start working towards a social work qualification through RTL.

Considerable attention is paid to recruitment. In places which have an employer partnership course, the union produces publicity which is then sent out in pay slips. In the case of a community-based course, the union sends promotional material to the homes of its members in the region. Normally, the union targets only those members in the lowest subscription bands, who tend to be the lowest paid and least well qualified. Leaflets, inviting members to "exploratory" meetings, are brief and allow for an expression of interest with very little commitment. At those meetings, options are discussed and study programmes drawn-up on an individual basis. Once a course has been run in a workplace or region, the union can start to rely on word-of-mouth recruitment.

Although they were initially offered as unaccredited programmes, most UNISON Open College courses now lead towards recognised qualifications. The director of education and training said: "We realised early on that most people wanted some form of accreditation, they appreciate the fact that they have earned something by their own efforts and that their achievement has been recognised. But it is for the individual to decide whether they take the course for its own sake or whether they want to work towards a certificate. Most of them do, but we don't decide that for them."

Outcomes

More than 6 000 union members had completed courses with UNISON Open College by the spring of 1998, and courses were attracting 2 000 new recruits every year. There was also considerable evidence to show that previously excluded or vulnerable groups were in the majority. An external evaluation of the first two years' intake showed that they came from a wide range of occupations, including catering, domestic work, manual work and nursing. While students were within a wide age range, from 21 to 65, the majority were over 35 and half over 45.

Nine out of ten recruits to the Open College had left school before the age of 16, six out of ten had no formal qualifications before joining the course and four out of ten were in part-time work. But the most revealing figure was that of average earning of the students: 76 per cent earned less than the Council of Europe's threshold for a reasonable living at the time of signing up for a course. Eight out of ten were women in very low-skill jobs. After just two years the college was reaching its intended audience.

Developing partnerships with employers has enabled the union to widen the scope of its activities and to make them more accessible. It has also involved the union in explaining and negotiating with employers in order to achieve support for a series of courses which had no immediate pay-off in the workplace. The work of the college has helped improve relations between individual employers and the unions. One UNISON Open College education officer said that employers initially feared that the offer from UNISON's education and training department might conceal a hidden agenda; one basis for these suspicions was the relatively low cost of union-provided education, compared with what employers normally spent on bought-in training. There were fears too that the union might be undermining the role of an employer's established training department. But the employers who finally signed partnership agreements found that the benefits of a more flexible, better educated workforce far outweighed their concerns about union activity, particularly at times of redundancy and rapid change in employment patterns.

Drop-out rates were far lower than for courses in mainstream institutions such as colleges, according to an independent study in 1996. More than eight out of ten participants completed their RTL course and six out of ten participants went on to other education and training. Almost a third (29 per cent) said they had been promoted, changed jobs or gained new responsibilities after taking the RTL course. Almost a quarter had taken on new responsibilities within UNISON, often to promote the work of the Open College. Some have decided to go further and train as teachers of further and adult education.

UNISON Open College has won national recognition: in 1996, when its Voluntary Education Adviser system won an Adult Learners' Week award; in 1997, the union won the Ford Award for work-based learning; and in 1998 a UNISON member won an individual learner's award. The programme was highlighted by the government in its Green Paper on lifelong learning, The Learning Age.

171|

Innovation and effectiveness

Several issues stand out in the UK studies:

– The University for Industry pilot has been very effective in reaching whole sectors of society – the elderly, unemployed and shift-workers – who previously felt excluded from adult learning and had therefore been vulnerable to wider exclusion.

– The UfI pilot was most innovative in providing the resources through a multitude of outlets to satisfy the immediate needs of learners who were afraid of returning to learn and would otherwise have dropped out.

– Priory Primary School was transformed from being a narrowly-focused institution to a resource for community development. Taking a highly original approach to parental support in school, staff turned the initiative into an adult learning opportunity.

– The UNISON Open College, in creating learning opportunities for thousands of adults, has also built bridges between employers and unions, boosting investment in general and vocational education to prevent social and economic exclusion.

– The projects overall were highly effective in tapping into traditional structures and institutions, in order to channel expertise, contacts and resources into the community.

Networks and the creation of new social capital have boosted the self-confidence of the disaffected, marginalised, vulnerable and excluded groups.

Commentary

The country has concentrated almost exclusively on issues of economic exclusion over the past two decades. The importance of investment in social capital and the concerns of the wider community have been neglected and at cost, not only to those individuals who have been marginalised through unemployment but to whole neighbourhoods.

An overwhelming message from the UK experience is that partnerships involving all the representative groups, from community associations and trade unions to the employer organisations and government (local and national), are essential for success in vocational training efforts to combat exclusion.

Adult learning as a weapon against exclusion is changing in the UK, as the three case studies illustrate. Indeed, adult education, like many of the people it serves, is being drawn back from the margins of the education service. Long-standing patterns have been broken at Priory Primary, to create a virtuous rather than vicious circle. The route to community school status, with a fully-fledged adult education service may have been a serendipitous outcome of efforts to raise pupil standards, but it is all the better for that and is a model that is worth closer attention.

The University for Industry pilot shows how important are partnership and a high public profile in sustaining an experimental programme. It still has a long way to go; there is a need to reach the wider group of adults – an estimated 6 million nationally – who have literacy problems. The question of reliable long-term funding is crucial in this respect.

UNISON's Open College is an acknowledged success story, and unique in the British trade union movement in having developed mass provision for individual rank and file members. This in a trade union dominated by part-time, low-paid and manual workers. Courses such as RTL have attracted large numbers of rank-and-file members into a generic education programme, saving many from redundancy, long-term unemployment and exclusion.

As was seen in the UNISON Open College, the UfI will depend on a more flexible approach from government and its funding agencies. The complex bureaucracy and wasteful duplication of effort among the various agencies which control the cash for further, higher and adult education remains, despite repeated pledges to cut red tape.

OECD 1999

Bibliography

Aprovechamientos Forestales de la Comunidad Indigena de Nuevo San Juan Parangaricutiro, Michoacan (1998),
"Resumen de Documento Base", Mimeo, Mexico.

CARNOY, M. and CASTELLS, M. (1997),
"Sustainable Flexibility: A Prospective Study on Work, Family and Society in the Information Age", mimeo, OECD, Paris.

Commission on Social Justice (1994),
Social Justice: Strategies for National Renewal, Vintage, London.

Conselho Nacional de Educaçao (1996),
"A Educaçao de Adultos em Portugal no Contexto da Educaçao ao Longo da Vida. Situaçao. Alternativas. Recomendaçoes. Parecer No. 1/96 (aprovado apos aprecioçao do projecto de parecer elaborado pelo Conselheiro José Ribeiro Dias), in Pareceres e Recomendaçoes, CNE, Lisboa, pp. 9-117.

Department for Education and Employment (1995),
Lifetime Learning: a consultation document; DfEE, London.

Department for Education and Employment (1998a),
The Learning Age: a renaissance for a new Britain, The Stationery Office Limited, London.

Department for Education and Employment (1998b),
University for Industry: engaging people in learning for life, Pathfinder Prospectus, DfEE, Sheffield.

Department of Trade and Industry (1995),
Competitiveness: Forging Ahead, Her Majesty's Stationery Office, London.

Fundación de Apoyo Infantil, Sonora (1998),
"Community Banks, Family Micro-Economy and Community Development", Mimeo, Mexico.

FIELD, J. (1996),
"Learning for Work: vocational education and training", in R. Fieldhouse (ed.), A History of Modern British Adult Education, National Institute of Adult Continuing Education, Leicester.

FIELD, J. (1998),
European Dimensions: Education, Training and the European Union, Jessica Kingsley, London.

HILLMAN, J. (1996),
University for Industry: creating a national learning network, Institute for Public Policy Research, London.

HILLS, J. (1998),
"Social Exclusion: the Content Behind the Babble", Social Sciences, Vol. 37, No. 2.

HIRSCH, D. (1997),
Social Protection and Inclusion: European challenges for the United Kingdom, Joseph Rowntree Charitable Trust, York.

HOUTCOOP, W. (1994),
"Competences and Qualifications in the Netherland: The Policy Context", Paper for the CEDFOP seminars on Competences, Amsterdam, 1993 and Marseilles, 1994, Max Goote Expert Centre, Amsterdam.

Instituto Nacional de Estadística, Geografía e Informática (1996),
Conteo de Poblacion y Vivienda 1995, INEGI, Aguascalientes Ags, Mexico.

ISTANCE, D., REES, G. and WILLIAMSON, H. (1994),
Young People not in Education, Training or Employment in South Glamorgan, South Glamorgan Training and Enterprise Council, Cardiff.

JANSEN, A.B. (1997),
De Demotieregeling van Wavin, OWASE, Handboek Loopbaanmanagement, aflevering 4.

KALLEN, D. (1998),
"Social Exclusion Old and New", Unpublished manuscript prepared for the OECD, Paris.

KENNEDY, H. (1997),
Learning Works: widening participation in further education, Further Education Funding Council, Coventry.

LIMA, L.C. (1996),
"Educaçao de Adultos e Construçao da Cidadania Democratica: Para uma critica do gerencialismo e da educaçao contabil", Inovaçao, No. 9, pp. 238-297.

MARTIN, S. and LOAEZA, E. (1997),
Mexico/United States Binational Study on Migration, Mexico Secretaria de Relaciones Exteriors, Mexico.

MELO, A., QUEIROS, A.M., SILVA, A. S., SALGADO, L., ROTHES, L., and RIBEIRO, M. (1998),
Uma Aposta Educativa na Participaçao de Todos. Documento de Estrategia para o Desenvolvimiento da Educaçao de Adultos, Ministerio da Educaçao, Lisboa.

MÉNDEZ, A. (1998),
"Capítulo 4. La formación de Educadores en el Programa Misiones Culturales", en Informe del Proyecto Educación de Adultos en Michoacán: Elementos para reorientar la práctica educativa y las formas de organización y gestión en comunidades rurales en situación de pobreza, CREFAL-SIMORELOS/CONACYT, mimeo, Mexico.

Ministerie van Onderwijs en Wetenschappen (1993),
"A Lifetime of Learning", Discussion Document, "The future development of adult education in its broadest sense", Ministerie van Onderwijs en Wetenschappen, Zoetermeer.

Ministerie van Sociale Zaken en Werkgelegenheid (1997),
"Sociale Nota 1998", Ministerie van Sociale Zaken en Werkgelegenheid, Den Haag.

Ministry of Education, Research & Church Affairs (1996),
"Reform 94 Administrative Services Department", Publications Division, Oslo.

Ministry of Education, Research & Church Affairs (1997),
"Reform 97 Administrative Services Department", Publications Division, Oslo.

OECD (1984),
Reviews of National Policies for Education: Portugal, Paris.

OECD (1990),
Reviews of National Policies for Education: Norway, Paris.

OECD (1991),
   Review of National Policies for Education: Netherlands, Paris.
OECD (1993),
   Reviews of National Policies for Education: Belgium, Paris.
OECD (1994),
   The OECD Jobs Study, Part I and II, Paris.
OECD (1996),
   OECD Economic Surveys: United Kingdom, Paris.
OECD (1997a),
   Reviews of National Policies for Education: Higher Education in Mexico; Paris.
OECD (1997b),
   OECD Economic Surveys: Belgium/Luxembourg, Paris.
OECD (1998a),
   Battle Against Exclusion – Social Assistance in Australia, Finland, Sweden and the United Kingdom, Vol. 1, Paris.
OECD (1998b),
   Battle Against Exclusion – Social Assistance in Belgium, the Czech Republic, the Netherlands and Norway, Vol. 2, Paris.
OECD (1998c),
   OECD Economic Surveys: Mexico, Paris.
OECD (1998d),
   OECD Economic Surveys: Netherlands, Paris.
OECD (1998e),
   OECD Economic Surveys: Norway, Paris.
OECD (1998f),
   OECD Economic Surveys: Portugal, Paris.
OECD (1998g),
   Education at a Glance – OECD Indicators, Paris.
OECD (1998h),
   Employment Outlook, Paris.
OECD (1998i),
   Implementing Inclusive Education, Paris.
OECD (1998j),
   Co-ordinating Services for Children and Youth at Risk – a World View, Paris.
OECD (1999),
   A Caring World: The new social policy agenda, Paris.
OECD and STATISTICS CANADA (1995),
   Literacy, Economy and Society. Results of the first International Adult Literacy Survey, Paris and Ottawa.
OECD and STATISTICS CANADA (1997),
   Literacy Skills for the Knowledge Society: Further Results of the International Adult Literacy Survey, Paris.
PIÑA, C. (1994),
   Educación y Trabajo. La experiencia de una empresa indígena, OEA-CREFAL, Mexico.

177

Royal Ministry of Churches, Education and Research (1994),
The Core Curriculum for Primary Schools, Secondary Schols and Adult Education in Norway, Akademika AS, Oslo.

SOHLMAN, A. (1998),
"The Culture of Adult Learning in Sweden", Paper from the April 1998 OECD Washington DC Conference on "How Adults Learn".

VAN DER KAMP, M. (1996),
"Participation: antecedent factors", in Tuijnman, A. (ed), *International Encyclopedia of Adult Education and Training*, 2nd. ed., Elsevier Science, Oxford, pp. 565-569.

VAN DAMME, V. and GOFFINEL, S.A. (1990),
Functional Literacy in Belgium, KBS-UNESCO Institute for Education, Brussel and Hamburg.

VAN DAMME, V., VAN DE POELE and VERHASSELT, E. (1997),
Hoe geletterd geciefered is Vlaaderen, Leuven-Amerstoot, Garant.

VAN DE KAMP, M. and SCHEEREN, J. (1996),
Functionele taal- en rekenvaardigheden van oudere volwassenen in Nederland, SVO-Project, GION, Groningen.

WALKER, R. and SHAW, A. (1998),
"Escaping from Social Assistance in Great Britain", in L. Liesering and R. Walker (eds.), *The Dynamics of Modern Society: Poverty, Policy and Welfare*, Policy Press, Bristol.

WAVIN NEDERLAND B.V. (1997),
Maatloopbaan, loopbaanombuigingsregeling, Hardenberg: Wavin Nederland B.V.

WETENSCHAPPELIJKE RAAD VOOR HET REGERINGSBELEID (1992),
Eigentijds burgerschap (Contemporary Citizenship), SDU, Den Haag.

OECD PUBLICATIONS, 2, rue André-Pascal, 75775 PARIS CEDEX
PRINTED IN FRANCE
(96 1999 03 1 P) ISBN 92-64-17026-X – No. 50569 1999